The Crook
in the Lot

The Crook in the Lot

Living with that thorn in your side

THOMAS BOSTON

INTRODUCTION BY J. I. PACKER

CHRISTIAN
HERITAGE

Scripture quotations are taken from the *King James Version*.

Scripture quotations marked NASB is taken from the New American Standard Bible®, Copyright © 1960, 1962, 1963, 1968, 1971, 1972, 1973, 1975, 1977, 1995 by The Lockman Foundation Used by Permission. (www.Lockman.org)

Introduction © J.I Packer 2002

© Christian Focus Publications, Ltd.

ISBN 978-1-84550-649-0

Published in 2002, reprinted in 2005 and 2012
by
Christian Focus Publications
Geanies House, Fearn,
Ross-shire, IV20 1TW, Scotland, United Kingdom

Cover design
by
Paul Lewis

Printed by
Bell and Bain, Glasgow

CONTENTS

INTRODUCTION

I

As an Englishman who has lived in North America for thirty-two years, during an era of rapid cultural change, I know more about how today's North Americans use words than I do about their British counterparts, so it may be that what I say in my next sentence would not apply so directly on the east side of the Atlantic. It is certain, however, that if a North American man in the street – say, the man on the Vancouver omnibus – heard a reference to the crook in the lot, he would think it must signify a criminal hiding out on a piece of probably undeveloped real estate (what Brits would call, property), and he would not be able to imagine what else it might mean. But in Thomas Boston's usage the *crook* is the crooked, that is the uncomfortable, discontenting aspects of a person's life, the things that the Puritans called losses and crosses, and that we speak of as the stones in our shoe, the thorns in our bed, the burrs under the saddle, and the complaints we have to live with; and the lot is the providentially appointed path that God sets each of his servants to travel. Boston, minister of Ettrick in south Scotland, who with Jonathan Edwards represents most brilliantly the prolonging into the eighteenth century of pure Puritanism, as a Bible-based, church-centred, faith-oriented, prayer-drenched movement of personal spiritual life, left at his death (he died in harness in 1732, aged 56) a little treatise on this theme, which he had already begun to prepare for the press. His friends finished the job, and the work was published in 1737, under the title *The Crook in the Lot: The Sovereignty and Wisdom of God in the Afflictions of Men Displayed.* That is what is before you now.

The movie *Shadowlands* represented C. S. Lewis as an inexperienced theorist who pontificated in public regarding pain and grief without knowing anything about it until he lost his wife. This, no doubt, was good Hollywood, but the story of the real C. S. Lewis was very different, and so was the story of Thomas Boston. *The Crook in the Lot* emerged from what in his autobiography Boston called 'the groaning part of my life', the final eight years, during which, in addition to ongoing battles for the gospel against the non-evangelical leadership of the Church of Scotland and the continuance of his wife's paralyzing depression, he was a martyr to some form of the stone (gravel, he called it) and saw himself become a physical wreck. When he wrote and spoke of life's troubles he knew what he was talking about, and the sense that this was so comes through strongly, even though there is nothing directly autobiographical in the analysis that the treatise offers.

It began, as the reader can see, as seven sermons: three on Ecclesiastes 7:13, 'Consider the work of God; for who can make that straight which he hath made crooked?'; one on Proverbs 16:19, 'Better is it to be of an humble spirit with the lowly, than to divide the spoil with the proud'; and three on 1 Peter 5:6: 'Humble yourselves therefore under the mighty hand of God, that he may exalt you in due time'. Boston had an architectural mind (Jonathan Edwards hailed him as 'a truly great divine'), and he liked preaching series of sermons that illustrated key topics from a number of texts; he wrote out the sermons in his easy, flowing English as part of his preparation for preaching them; and here, as in his better-known *Fourfold State*, the combination of perfect clarity with biblical light and weight searches the reader's heart and again and again makes us face ourselves on specific matters, impacting us with the sudden force of a depth-charge that explodes far below the surface level of our being. This is a way of saying that, as with Edwards and many of the Puritans of the previous century, divine unction rests on Boston's homiletical writing just as once it rested on his actual preaching; and that is a way of saying that the reality of the power of God in his own heart spilled over into his verbal communication. Be prepared, then, to find that God is preaching to you through Boston as you read *The Crook in the Lot*.

II

Two years before his death Boston wrote: 'I bless my God in Jesus Christ, that ever he made me a Christian, and took an early dealing with my soul [Boston came to faith at age eleven, under the preaching of Henry Erskine, a minister ejected from the Church of England in 1662], that ever he made me a minister of the gospel, and gave me true insight into the doctrine of his grace.' That 'true insight' which *The Crook in the Lot* presupposes, can be learned in detail from

Boston's voluminous though very self-consistent output, studied as a whole; or from the Westminster Confession and Catechisms, where it is crystallized'; but modern readers may not have time or inclination for this research, and their minds may already be possessed by different notions. So before going further I shall sketch out the frame of doctrine into which this little treatise fits. It is doctrine with a catechetical rather than an academic cast, in other words it is truth as one presents it to persons ignorant of Christianity in order to bring them to know, love, worship and serve God, and thus to make them true disciples of Jesus Christ.

1. The triune God, through whom we exist, in whose hands we always are, and who will in due course judge us and award us our final destiny, is totally sovereign over everything in his world, controlling even the free choices of human beings.

2. The human heart is naturally self-centred, self-deifying, self-serving, and unresponsive and hostile to God's claims, so that it leads everyone to live in a way which, if not changed, will bring final condemnation, rejection, retribution and separation from God's fellowship and love.

3. Jesus Christ, the incarnate Lord and Mediator, prophet, priest and king, crucified, risen and reigning, offers himself to everyone in the gospel, inviting and commanding all who hear to receive and trust him as the Saviour, Lord and Friend in and through whom they may be forgiven, and restored, and adopted into the Father's family for transformation into the image of the Son.

4. Through regeneration of heart by the Holy Spirit persons who seek Christ find him, and by faith live new

lives henceforth as his disciples, empowered by the Spirit who now endwells them.

5. In every disciple's life there are crooked things, unpleasant and unwelcome, which God uses to test us, strengthen us, humble us, correct us, teach us lessons, further our self-knowledge, repentance, and sanctity, shield us from greater evils, and thus bring us blessing, grievous as at first sight the crooked things seem to be.

6. The knowledge that in every case the crook in our lot belongs to this world only, and that again and again God delivers his people when they pray from particular afflictions that burden them here and now, should sustain believers as they undergo these divine chastenings, helping them to hold fast the certainty that 'all things work together for good for those who love God, who are called according to his purpose' (Rom. 8:28, NRSV).

These are the basic truths of which, at least in rough terms, Boston expects his readers to have some awareness. His treatise will remind us of many of them and amplify some of them in detail, but none is presented as a new idea, and evidently Boston sees his role as helping people to know better, and apply to themselves more thoroughly, things that in some sense they know already. Some of Boston's thoughts may be new to us, but that does not mean they were new to his own first hearers. It is clear that at catechetical level congregations were better taught in Boston's day than they are in ours – which, when you think of the way catechizing has dropped out of church and family life, is hardly matter for surprise.

With these truths clear in our minds, however, we are equipped to tune in to *The Crook in the Lot* and, if I may put it this way, to suck sweetness out of it.

11

III

To this end I pose two questions.

First: what did Boston design the *Crook* to do, originally to his hearers at Ettrick and then to his readers, people such as ourselves? To what end did he select and arrange this material? What, pastorally, was his aim? Long ago I was taught that if you aim at nothing in particular you are sure to achieve it. What did Boston hope to achieve?

A partial answer would be: to teach people. It has been said that the three priorities in pastoral ministry are, first, to teach, second, to teach, and third, to teach, and Boston would have agreed with that. Preaching, as persons like himself in the Puritan tradition understood it, is teaching plus application, and the application is itself a didactic engagement of the mind before it is anything else. The rationale of this position is that all truth enters the heart via the understanding, and that authentic Christianity is essentially belief of and obedience to the revealed truth of God, and that the Bible itself is that truth, presented in a variety of forms – by narrative, by parable, by argumentation, by vision, and so on – but all, as Paul says, 'profitable for teaching, for reproof, for correction, for training in righteousness' (2 Tim. 3:16, NASB). Boston's teaching process enlarges biblical understanding in more than one way; the passages he gathers illuminate the truth they are cited to support, and that truth in turn illuminates the significance of these passages in their own context. The modern way to mark this fact is to applaud Boston for his skill in canonical interpretation, that is, his insight into the whole Bible, all 66 books of it in the two testamentary collections, as a theological unity setting forth in a wonderfully consistent and coherent manner the will, work and ways of God the Creator-become-Redeemer, plus the wisdom about God, the world, and life that the godly are called to learn. Like Calvin and the Puritans before him, Boston offers canonical interpretation of the Bible that in both spiritual and intellectual quality far outstrips most ventures in this field today. One supposes that depth of dependence on the Holy Spirit, who as inspirer of the Bible must ever be its ultimate interpreter, has something to do with this fact.

Boston's basic contention, which all his teaching here is concerned to make good, is that: 'A just view of afflicting incidents is altogether necessary to a Christian deportment under them; and that view is to be obtained only by faith, not by sense; for it is the ... Word alone that represents them justly, discovering in them the work of God, and consequently, designs becoming the divine perfections.' Assuming general knowledge of the plan of salvation as laid out above, he first shows us with piercing precision what constitutes a crook in one's lot (circumstances causing revulsion and complaint, and generating all the temptations of discontent), and he analyzes for us what modes of crook there are (defects in our make up; dishonour, sometimes observed, sometimes not; lack of appropriate success in our endeavours; and bad relationships everywhere). Then he tells us how we should seek God's help to 'even' (straighten) the crooks, while humbling ourselves under them and ac-knowledging that some of them are here to stay while this life lasts. And finally he explains how we should focus our hope on the promised 'lifting up' that, here or hereafter, will be our experience. Points recur in different connections as he moves along, in a way that makes one think of the spiral

13

tunnels whereby trains in Switzerland and Western Canada gain height. The trains emerge almost directly above where they went in, but much higher up; and similarly the reappearances of Boston's points, slightly reangled and newly illustrated as they usually are, raise our understanding of them higher each time we meet them. First to last, Boston gives us masterful teaching, with what Americans describe as 'review' and Brits call 'revision' built in.

But that is not all that Boston aims to do. Teaching is the means to his end, rather than the end itself. His goal, like that of every other real preacher, is to change those he addresses, or at least to see them changed by the power of God. Here, along with his permanent purpose of leading the unconverted to faith and the new birth, his clear purpose is to discipline Christ's disciples in reverent, realistic, hope-filled humility, as they face up to the inescapable imperfections of life in general and their own lives in particular. He wants us to be utterly sure of the wisdom and goodness of God's Providence as we adjust to the disappointments, deprivations and limitations of our lives, and to glorify God by the way we cope with them. He is consciously ministering to the many who he knows are not strong at this point, seeking to establish them in humble, prayerful steadiness. His book is preaching on paper, and if it left its readers unmoved and unchanged he would certainly count it a failure – a crook in his own lot, we might say.

IV

That brings us to my second question. Has this book a message for today? The answer, I believe, is yes, most certainly; but it is a message that moderns are likely to find very hard to hear. Why? Let me explain.

Psychologists and philosophers have noticed that it is common for people to have in their minds incompatible lines of thought, desire, valuation, expectation and purpose, and to be unaware of the incompatibility. They call this condition cognitive dissonance. Pastorally, the insight is important, for the mixture of faith and unbelief, wisdom and foolishness, spiritual discernment and spiritual myopia, that we find in all believers in this world, virtually guarantees that there will be *cognitive dissonance* in Christian minds – self-contradiction and incoherence, that is – over and over again with regard to the things of God. So it proves to be, and pastors are constantly having to detect and correct mistakes of this kind.

Now, one particular form of cognitive dissonance that is widespread today among evangelical Protestants (interestingly, you do not find it among Roman Catholics and Orthodox) is as follows. Nobody questions that Christ tells his followers to deny themselves – that is, to give to God all the personal hopes and dreams they have cherished, and accept that non-fulfilment of these may be part of his plan – and to take up their cross – that is, be willing to become discredited outcasts, like the condemned men whose ranks Jesus was to join who were made to carry the means of their crucifixion to the place appointed for it. This is a clear, sober warning from our Lord that discipleship will have its downs as well as its ups, its distresses as well as its delights, and no Christian challenges it. But at the same time the comfort-oriented materialism of our age urges that painless, trouble-free living is virtually a human right, and against this background many who believe they believe let themselves think that because they are God's children they will always be shielded from major troubles, such as strike other people, and will be led through life on a pain-free path, with all pleasant things provided, as would happen on a cruise. The brash and simplistic expression of this syndrome is found in the health and wealth gospel of some televangelists; the more reflective and sophisticated expression of it appears in the pained question, voiced when trauma comes – bereavement, betrayal, incurable disease, business collapse, or whatever – 'How could God let this happen to me?' and it further appears in the theological theories that say God would have stopped it if he could, but he couldn't, because his sovereignty is limited. Here we meet cognitive dissonance, anchored deep in people's hearts. The fantasy of nasty things kept at bay and only nice things meant for us here and now dies hard, and where it has not yet died Boston's realism, bracing, clarifying and stabilizing as it is, will not be received.

But be that as it may, the pure biblical wisdom of *The Crook in the Lot* is badly needed by many of us, and so I am delighted that it is being made available again in this handy form. And I hope that what I have written here will help a new generation to read it with understanding and gratitude to God. For truly, as Americans love to say, this is where it's at.

J. I. Packer

1

The Sovereignty and Wisdom of God in Man's Affliction

Consider the work of God: for who can make that straight which he hath made crooked?
Ecclesiastes 7:13

A just view of afflicting incidents is altogether necessary to a Christian deportment under them; and that view is to be obtained only by faith, not by sense; for, it is the light of the word alone that represents them justly, discovering in them the work of God, and, consequently, designs becoming the divine perfections. When these are perceived by the eye of faith, and duly considered, we have a just view of afflicting incidents, fitted to quell the turbulent motions of corrupt affections under dismal outward appearances.

It is under this view that Solomon, in the preceding part of this chapter, advances several paradoxes, which are surprising determinations in favour of certain things, that, to the eye of sense, looking gloomy and hideous, are therefore generally reputed grievous and shocking. He pronounces the day of one's death to be better than the day of his birth; namely, the day of the death of one, who having become the friend of God through faith, has led a life to the honour of God, and service of his generation, and thereby raised himself the good and savoury name better than precious ointment (v. 1). In like manner, he pronounces the house of mourning to be preferable to the house of feasting, sorrow to laughter, and a wise man's rebuke to a fool's song; for that, howbeit the latter are indeed the more pleasant, yet the former are the more profitable (vv. 2-6). And observing with concern, how men are in hazard, not only from the world's frowns and ill-usage, oppression making a wise man mad, but also from its smiles and caresses, a gift destroying the heart; therefore, since whatever way it goes there is danger, he pronounces the end of every worldly thing better than the beginning thereof (vv. 7, 8). And from the whole, he justly infers, that it is better to be humble and patient, than proud and impatient, under afflicting dispensations; since, in the former case, we wisely submit to what is really best; in the latter, we fight against it (v. 8). And he dissuades from being angry with our lot, because of the adversity found therein (v. 9); cautions against making odious comparisons of former and present times, in that point insinuating undue reflections on the Providence of God (v. 10): and, against that querulous and fretful disposition, he first prescribes a general remedy, namely, holy wisdom, as that which enables us to make the best of every thing, and even gives life in killing circumstances (vv. 11, 12); and then a particular remedy, consisting in a due application of that wisdom, towards taking a just view of the case, 'Consider the work of God: for who can make that straight which he hath made crooked?'

In which words are proposed, 1. The remedy itself; 2. The suitableness thereof.

1. The remedy itself, is a wise eyeing [consideration] of the hand of God in all we find to bear hard upon us:

18

'Consider the work (or, see thou the doing) of God', namely, in the crooked, rough, and disagreeable parts of thy lot, the crosses thou find in it. You see very well the cross itself; yea, you turn it over and over in the mind, and leisurely view it on all sides: you look, withal, to this and the other second cause of it, and so you are in a foam and fret. But, [if] would you be quiet and satisfied in the matter, lift up your eyes towards heaven, see the doing of God in it, the operation of his hand. Look at that, and consider it well; eye [consider] the first cause of the crook in your lot; behold how it is the work of God, his doing.

2. This view of the crook in our lot is very suitable to still indecent risings of heart, and quiet us under it: 'for who can (that is none can) make that straight which God hath made crooked?' As to the crook in thy lot, God hath made it; and it must continue while he will have it so. Should you ply your utmost force to even it, or make it straight, your attempt will be vain: it will not alter for all thou canst do; only he who made it can mend it, or make it straight. This consideration, this view of the matter, is a proper means, at once, to silence and to satisfy men, and so to bring them unto a dutiful submission to their Maker and Governor, under the crook in their lot.

Now, we take up the purpose of the text in these three propositions.

I: Whatsoever crook there is in one's lot, it is of God's making.

II: What God sees meet to mar, no one shall be able to mend in his lot.

III: The considering of the crook in the lot as the work of God, or of his making, is a proper means to bring us to a Christian deportment under it.

Proposition I: Whatsoever crook there is in one's lot, it is of God's making.

Here, two things are to be considered, namely, the crook itself, and God's making of it.

I. As to the crook itself, the crook in the lot, for the better understanding thereof, these few things that follow are premised.

1. There is a certain train or course of events, by the Providence of God, falling to every one of us during our life in this world: and that is our lot, as being allotted to us by the sovereign God, our Creator and Governor, 'in whose hand our breath is, and whose are all our ways'. This train of events is widely different to different persons, according to the will and pleasure of the sovereign manager, who orders men's conditions in the world in a great variety, some moving in a higher, some in a lower sphere.

2. In that train or course of events, some fall out cross to us, and against the grain; and these make the crook in our lot. While we are here, there will be cross events, as well as agreeable ones, in our lot and condition. Sometimes things are softly and agreeably gliding on; but, by and by, there is some incident which alters that course, grates us, and pains us, as when we have made a wrong step, we begin to halt.

3. Every body's lot in this world hath some crook in it. Complainers are apt to make odious comparisons: they look about, and taking a distant view of the condition of others, can discern nothing in it but what is straight, and just to one's wish; so they pronounce their neighbours' lot wholly straight. But that is a false verdict; there is no perfection here; no lot out of heaven without a crook. For, as to 'all the works that are done under the sun, behold all is vanity and vexation of spirit. That which is crooked cannot be made

straight' (Eccles. 1:14, 15). Who would not have thought that Haman's lot was very straight, while his family was in a flourishing condition, and he prospering in riches and honour, being prime minister of state in the Persian court, and standing high in the king's favour? Yet there was, at the same time, a crook in his lot, which so galled him, that 'all this availed him nothing' (Esther 5:13). Every one feels for himself, where he is pinched, though others perceive it not. Nobody's lot, in this world, is wholly crooked; there are always some straight and even parts in it. Indeed, when men's passions, having got up, have cast a mist over their minds, they are ready to say, all is wrong with them, nothing right; but, though in hell that tale is true, and ever will be so, yet it is never true in this world; for there, indeed, there is not a drop of comfort allowed (Luke 16:24, 25) but here it always holds good, that 'it is of the Lord's mercies we are not consumed' (Lam. 3:22).

4. The crook in the lot came into the world by sin: it is owing to the fall (Rom. 5:12). 'By one man sin entered into the world, and death by sin'; under which death, the crook in the lot is comprehended, as a state of comfort or prosperity is, in scripture style, expressed by living (1 Sam. 25:6; John 4:50, 51). Sin so bowed the hearts and minds of men, that they became crooked in respect of the holy law; and God justly so bowed their lot, that it became crooked too. And this crook in our lot inseparably follows our sinful condition, till, dropping this body of sin and death, we get within heaven's gates.

These being premised, a crook in the lot speaks in general, two things, (1) Adversity, (2) Continuance. Accordingly, it makes a day of adversity, opposed to the day of prosperity, in the verse immediately following the text.

21

The crook in the lot is, first, some one or other piece of adversity. The prosperous part of one's lot, which goes forward according to one's wish, is the straight and even part of it; the adverse part, going a contrary way, is the crooked part thereof. God hath intermixed these two in men's condition in this world; that, as there is some prosperity therein, making the straight line, so there is also some adversity, making the crooked: which mixture hath place, not only in the lot of saints, who are told, that 'in the world they shall have tribulation', but even in the lot of all, as already observed. Secondly, it is adversity of some continuance. We do not reckon it a crooked thing, which, though forcibly bended and bowed together, yet presently recovers its former straightness. There are twinges of the rod of adversity, which passing like a stitch in one's side, all is immediately set to rights again: one's lot may be suddenly overclouded, and the cloud vanish ere he is aware. But under the crook, one having leisure to find his smart, is in some concern to get the crook made even. So the crook in the lot is adversity, continued for a shorter or longer time.

Now, there is a threefold crook in the lot incident to the children of men.

1. One made by a cross dispensation, which, howsoever in itself passing, yet hath lasting effects. Such a crook did Herod's cruelty make in the lot of the mothers in Bethlehem, who by the murderers were left 'weeping for their slain children, and would not be comforted, because they were not' (Matt. 2:18). A slip of the foot may soon be made, which will make a man go halting long after. 'As the fishes are taken in an evil net: so are the sons of men snared in an evil time' (Eccles. 9:12). The thing may fall

22

out in a moment, under which the party shall go halting to the grave.

2. There is a crook made by a train of cross dispensations, whether of the same or different kinds, following hard one upon another, and leaving lasting effects behind them. Thus in the case of Job, while one messenger of evil tidings was yet speaking, another came (Job 1:16-18). Cross events coming one upon the neck of another, deep calling unto deep, make a sore crook. In that case, the party is like unto one, who, recovering his sliding foot from one shaky piece of ground, sets it on another equally shaky, which immediately gives way under him too. Or, like unto one, who, travelling in an unknown mountainous track, after having, with difficulty, made his way over one mountain, is expecting to see the plain country; but, instead thereof, there comes in view, time after time, a new mountain to be passed. This crook in Asaph's lot had like to have made him give up all his religion, until he went into the sanctuary, where this mystery of Providence was unfolded to him (Ps. 73:13-17). Solomon observes, 'That there be just men, unto whom it happeneth according to the work of the wicked' (Eccles. 8:14). Providence taking a run against them, as if they were to be run down for good and all. Whoever they be, whose life in no part thereof affords them experience of this, sure Joseph missed not of it in his young days, nor Jacob in his middle days, nor Peter in his old days, nor our Saviour all his days.

3. There is a crook made by one cross dispensation, with lasting effects thereof coming in the room of another removed. Thus one crook straightened, there is another made in its place: and so there is still a crook. Want [lack] of children had long been the crook in Rachel's lot (Gen. 30:1).

That was at length made even to her mind; but then she got another in its stead, hard labour in travailing to bring forth (35:16). This world is a wilderness, in which we may indeed get our station changed; but the result will be out of one wilderness station [and] into another. When one part of the lot is made even, soon some other part thereof will be crooked.

More particularly, the crook in the lot hath in it four things of the nature of that which is crooked.

Disagreeableness

A crooked thing is wayward; and, being laid to a rule, answers it not, but declines from it. There is not, in any body's lot, any such thing as a crook, in respect of the will and purposes of God. Take the most harsh and dismal dispensation in one's lot, and lay it to the eternal decree, made in the depth of infinite wisdom, before the world began, and it will answer it exactly, without the least deviation, 'all things being wrought after the counsel of his will' (Eph. 1:11). Lay it to the providential will of God, in the government of the world, and there is a perfect harmony - if Paul is to be bound at Jerusalem, and 'delivered unto the hands of the Gentiles', it is 'the will of the Lord it should be so' (Acts 21:11, 14). Wherefore, the greatest crook of the lot on Earth, is straight in heaven: there is no disagreeableness in it there. But in every person's lot there is a crook in respect of their mind and natural inclination. The adverse dispensation lies cross to that rule, and will by no means answer it, nor harmonize with it. When Divine Providence lays one to the other, there is a manifest disagreeableness: the man's will goes one way, and the dispensation another way: the will bends upwards, and cross events press down:

so they are contrary. And there, and only there, lies the crook. It is this disagreeableness which makes the crook in the lot fit matter of trial and exercise to us, in this our state of probation: in which, if thou wouldst approve thyself to God, walking by faith, not by sight, thou must quiet thyself in the will and purpose of God, and not insist that it should be according to thy mind (Job 35:33).

Unsightliness

Crooked things are unpleasant to the eye: and no crook in the lot seems to be joyous, but grievous, making an unsightly appearance (Heb. 12:11). Therefore men need to beware of giving way to their thoughts, to dwell on the crook in their lot, and of keeping it too much in view. David shows a hurtful experience of his, in that kind, Psalm 39:3. 'While I was musing the fire burned.' Jacob acted a wiser part, called his youngest son Benjamin, the son of the right-hand, whom the dying mother had named Benoni, *the son of my sorrow;* by this means providing, that the crook in his lot should not be set afresh in his view, on every occasion of mentioning the name of his son. Indeed, a Christian may safely take a steady and leisurely view of the crook of his lot in the light of the holy word, which represents it as the discipline of the covenant. So faith will discover a hidden beauty in it, under a very unsightly outward appearance. Perceiving the suitableness thereof to the infinite goodness, love, and wisdom of God, and to the real and most valuable interests of the party; by which means one comes to take pleasure, and that a most refined pleasure, in distresses (2 Cor. 12:10). But whatever the crook in the lot be to the eye of faith, it is not at all pleasant to the eye of sense.

Unfitness for motion

Solomon observes the cause of the uneasy and ungraceful walking of the lame (Prov. 26:7). 'The legs of the lame are not equal.' This uneasiness they find, who are exercised about the crook in their lot: a high spirit and a low adverse lot, makes great difficulty in the Christian walk. There is nothing that gives temptation greater access, than the crook in the lot; nothing more apt to occasion out-of-the-way steps. Therefore, says the apostle (Heb. 12:13), 'Make straight paths for your feet, lest that which is lame be turned out of the way'. They who are labouring under it are to be pitied then, and not to be rigidly censured; though they are rare persons who learn this lesson, till taught by their own experience. It is long since Job made an observation in this case, which holds good unto this day (Job 12:5) 'He that is ready to slip with his feet is as a lamp despised in the thought of him that is at ease'.

> 'Aptness to catch hold and entangle, like hooks, fish-hooks' (Amos 4:2).

The crook in the lot doth so very readily make impression, to the ruffling and fretting one's spirit, irritating corruption, that Satan fails not to make diligent use of it for these dangerous purposes; which point once gained by the tempter, the tempted, ere he is aware, finds himself entangled as in a thicket, out of which he knows not how to extricate himself. In that temptation it often proves like a crooked stick, troubling a standing pool, which not only raises up the mud all over, but brings up from the bottom some very ugly thing. Thus it brought up a spice of blasphemy and atheism in Asaph's case (Ps. 73:13), 'Verily I have cleansed my heart in vain, and washed my hands in innocence'. As if he had said, 'There is nothing at all in religion, it is a vain and empty thing that profits nothing; I was a fool to have been in care about purity and holiness, whether of heart or life. Ah! Is this the pious Asaph? How is he turned so quite unlike himself!' But the crook in the lot is a handle, whereby the tempter makes surprising discoveries of latent corruption even in the best.

This is the nature of the crook in the lot; let us now observe what part of the lot it falls in. Three conclusions may be established upon this head.

It may fall in any part of the lot; there is no exempted one in the case: for, sin being found in every part, the crook may take place in any part. Being 'all as an unclean thing, we may all fade as a leaf' (Isa. 64:6). The main stream of sin, which the crook readily follows, runs in very different channels, in the case of different persons. And in regard of the various dispositions of the minds of men, that will prove a sinking weight unto one, which another would go very lightly under.

It may at once fall into many parts of the lot, the Lord calling, as in a solemn day, one's terrors round about (Lam. 2:22). Sometimes God makes one notable crook in a man's lot; but its name may be Gad, being but the forerunner of a troop which cometh. Then the crooks are multiplied, so that the party is made to halt on each side. While one stream, let in from one quarter, is running full against him, another is let in on him from another quarter, till in the end the waters break in on every hand.

It often falls in the tender part; I mean, that part of the lot wherein one is least able to bear it, or, at least thinks he is so. Psalm 4:12, 13: 'It was not an enemy that reproached me, then I could have borne it. But it was thou, a man,

27

mine equal, my guide, and mine acquaintance'. If there is any one part of the lot, which of all others one is disposed to nestle in, the thorn will readily be laid there, especially if he belongs to God; in that thing wherein he is least of all able to be touched, he will be sure to be pressed. There the trial will be taken of him; for there is the grand competition with Christ. 'I take from them the desires of their eyes, and that whereupon they set their minds' (Ezek. 24:25). Since the crook in the lot is the special trial appointed for every one, it is altogether reasonable, and becoming the wisdom of God, that it fall on that which of all things doth most rival him.

Afflictions common to mankind.
But more particularly, the crook may be observed to fall in these four parts of the lot.

In the natural part affecting persons considered as of the make allotted for them by the great God that formed all things. The parents of mankind, Adam and Eve, were formed altogether sound and entire, without the least blemish, whether in soul or body; but in the formation of their posterity, there often appears a notable variation from the original. Bodily defects, superfluities, deformities, infirmities, natural or accidental, make the crook in the lot of some: they have something unsightly or grievous about them. Crooks of this kind, more or less observable, are very common and ordinary; the best are not exempted from them; and it is purely owing to sovereign pleasure they are not more numerous. Tender eyes made the crook in the lot of Leah (Gen. 29:17). Rachel's beauty was balanced with barrenness, the crook in her lot (ch. 30:1). Paul, the great apostle of the Gentiles, was, it should seem, no personable man, but of a mean outward appearance, for which fools were apt to condemn him (2 Cor. 10:10). Timothy was of a weak and sickly frame (1 Tim. 5:23). And there is a yet far more considerable crook in the lot of the lame, the blind, the deaf, and the dumb. Some are weak to a degree in their intellects; and it is the crook in the lot of several bright souls to be overcast with clouds, notably clouded and darkened, from the crazy bodies in which they are lodged. An eminent instance whereof we have in the grave, wise, and patient Job, 'going mourning without the sun; yea, standing up and crying in the congregation' (Job 30:28).

Reputation.
It may fall in the honorary part. There is an honour due to all men, the small as well as the great (1 Pet. 2:17), and that upon the ground of the original constitution of human nature, as it was framed in the image of God. But, in the sovereign disposal of holy Providence, the crook in the lot of some falls here; they are neglected and slighted; their credit is still kept low; they go through the world under a cloud, being put into an ill name, their reputation sunk. This sometimes is the natural consequence of their own foolish and sinful conduct; as in the case of Dinah, who, by her gadding abroad [idle wandering] to satisfy her youthful curiosity, regardless of, and therefore not waiting for a providential call, brought a lasting stain on her honour (Gen. 34). But, where the Lord intends a crook of this kind in one's lot, innocence will not be able to ward it off in an ill-natured world; neither will true merit be able to make head against it, to make one's lot stand straight in that part. Thus David represents his case, Psalm 31:11-13: 'They that did see me without, fled from me: I am forgotten as a dead

29

man out of mind: I am like a broken vessel. For I have heard the slander of many.'

Thirdly, It may fall in the vocational part. Whatever is a man's calling or station in the world, be it sacred or civil, the crook in their lot may take its place therein. Isaiah was an eminent prophet, but most unsuccessful (Isa. 53:1). Jeremiah met with such a train of discouragements and ill usage in the exercise of his sacred function, that he was very near giving it up, saying, 'I will not make mention of him, nor speak any more in his name' (Jer. 20:9). The Psalmist observes this crook often to be made in the lot of some men very industrious in their civil business who sow in the fields - and at times 'God blesseth them - and suffereth not their cattle to decrease: but again, they are minished, and brought low, through oppression, affliction and sorrow' (Ps. 107:37-39). Such a crook was made in Job's lot after he had long stood even. Some manage their employments with all care and diligence; the husbandman carefully working his ground; the sheep-master 'diligent to know the state of his flocks, and looking well to his herds'; the tradesman, early and late at his business; the merchant, diligently plying his, watching and falling in with the most fair and promising opportunities; but there is such a crook in that part of their lot, as all they are able to do can by no means make even. For why? The most proper means used for compassing an end are insignificant without a word of divine appointment commanding their success. 'Who is he that saith, and it cometh to pass, when the Lord commandeth it not?' (Lam. 3:37). People ply their business with skill and industry, but the wind turns in their face. Providence crosses their enterprises, disconcerts their measures, frustrates their hopes and expectations, renders their endeavours unsuccessful, and so puts and keeps them still in straitened circumstances. 'So the race is not to the swift, nor the battle to the strong, neither yet bread to the wise' (Eccles.9:11). Providence interposing, crooks the measures which human prudence and industry had laid straight towards the respective ends; so the swift lose the race, and the strong the battle, and the wise miss of bread; while, in the mean time, some one or other providential incident, supplying the defect of human wisdom, conduct, and ability, the slow gain the race and carry the prize; the weak win the battle and enrich themselves with the spoil; and bread falls into the lap of the fool.

Relationships.

It may fall in the relational part. Relations are the joints of society; and there the crook in the lot may take place, one's smartest pain being often felt in these joints. They are in their nature the springs of man's comfort; yet, they often turn the greatest bitterness to him. Sometimes this crook is occasioned by the loss of relations. Thus a crook was made in the lot of Jacob, by means of the death of Rachel, his beloved wife, and the loss of Joseph, his son and darling, which had like to have made him go halting to the grave. Job laments this crook in his lot, 'Thou hast made desolate all my company'(Job 16:7). Meaning his dear children, every one of whom he had laid in the grave, not so much as one son or daughter left him. Again, sometimes it is made through the afflicting hand of God lying heavy on them: which, in virtue of their relation, recoils on the party, as is feelingly expressed by that believing woman (Matt. 15:22), 'Have mercy on me, O Lord; my daughter is grievously vexed'. Ephraim felt the smart of family afflictions, 'when

31

he called his son's name Beriah, because it went evil with his house' (1 Chron. 7:23). Since all is not only vanity, but vexation of spirit, it can hardly miss, but the more of these springs of comfort are opened to a man, he must, at one time or other, find he has but the more sources of sorrows to gush out and spring in upon him; the sorrow always proportioned to the comfort found in them, or expected from them. And, finally, the crook is sometimes made here by their proving uncomfortable through the disagreeableness of their temper and disposition. There was a crook in Job's lot, by means of an undutiful, ill-natured wife (Job 19:17). In Abigail's, by means of a surly, ill-tempered husband (1 Sam. 25:25). In Eli's, through the perverseness and obstinacy of his children (2:25). In Jonathan's, through the furious temper of his father (20:30-33). So do men oftentimes find their greatest cross, where they expected their greatest comfort. Sin hath unhinged the whole creation, and made every relation susceptible of the crook. In the family are found masters hard and unjust, servants froward and unfaithful; in a neighbourhood, men selfish and uneasy; in the church, unedifying ministers offensive in their walk, and people contemptuous and disorderly, a burden to the spirits of ministers. In the state, oppressive magistrates, opposers of that which is good, and subjects turbulent and seditious; all these cause crooks in the lot of their relatives. And thus far of the [type of] crook itself.

God's Sovereignty in all Affliction.

II. Having seen the crook itself, we are in the next place, to consider of God's making it.

And here [it] is to be shown A. It is of God's making. B. How it is of his making. C. Why he makes it.

A. That the crook in the lot, whatever it is, is of God's making appears from these three considerations.

It cannot be questioned, but the crook in the lot, considered as a crook, is a penal evil, whatever it is for the matter thereof; that is, whether the thing in itself, its immediate cause and occasion, be sinful or not, it is certainly a punishment or affliction. Now, as it may be, as such, holily and justly brought on us, by our Sovereign Lord and Judge, so he expressly claims the doing or making of it, Amos 3:6: 'Shall there be evil in a city, and the Lord has not done it?' Wherefore, since there can be no penal evil, but of God's making, and the crook in the lot is such an evil, it is necessarily concluded to be of God's making.

It is evident, from the scripture doctrine of divine Providence, that God brings about every man's lot, and all the parts thereof. He sits at the helm of human affairs, and turns them about whithersoever he listeth. 'Whatsoever the Lord pleased, that did he in heaven and in earth, in the seas and all deep places' (Ps. 135:6). There is not any thing whatsoever befalls us, without his overruling hand. The same Providence that brought us out of the womb, brings us to, and fixes us in the condition and place allotted for us, by him who 'hath determined the times, and the bounds of our habitation' (Acts 17:26). It overrules the smallest and most casual things about us, such as 'hairs of our head falling on the ground' (Matt. 10:29, 30); 'A lot cast into the lap' (Prov. 16:33). Yea the free acts of our will, whereby we choose for ourselves, for even 'the king's heart is in the hand of the Lord, as the rivers of water' (Prov. 21:1). And the whole steps we make, and which others make in reference to us; for 'the way of man is not in himself; it is not man that walketh to direct his steps' (Jer. 10:23). And this, whether these steps causing the crook be deliberate and sinful ones, such as Joseph's brethren selling him into Egypt; or whether they be undesigned, such as manslaughter purely casual, as when one hewing wood, kills his neighbour with 'the head of the axe slipping from the helve' (Deut. 19:5). For there is a holy and wise Providence that governs the sinful and the heedless actions of men, as a rider doth a lame horse, of whose halting, not he, but the horse's lameness, is the true and proper cause; wherefore in the former of these cases, God is said to have sent Joseph into Egypt (Gen. 45:7), and in the latter, to deliver one into his neighbour's hand (Exod. 21:13).

God has, by an eternal decree, immoveable as mountains of brass (Zech. 6:1), appointed the whole of every one's lot, the crooked parts thereof, as well as the straight. By the same eternal decree, whereby the high and low parts of the earth, the mountains and the valleys, were appointed, are the heights and the depths, the prosperity and adversity, in the lot of the inhabitants thereof determined, and they are brought about, in time, in a perfect agreeableness thereto.

The mystery of Providence, in the government of the world, is, in all the parts thereof, the building reared up of God, in exact conformity to the plan in his decree, 'who worketh all things after the counsel of his own will' (Eph. 1:11). So that there is never a crook in one's lot, but may be run up to this original. Hereof Job piously sets us an example in his own case, 'He is in one mind, and who can turn him? and what his soul desireth, even that he doth. For he performeth the thing that is appointed for me; and many such things are with him' (Job 18:13, 14).

How God Afflicts.
That we may see how the crook in the lot is of God's making, we must distinguish between pure sinless crooks, and impure sinful ones.

First, There are pure and sinless crooks; which are mere afflictions, cleanly crosses, grievous indeed, but not defiling. Such was Lazarus's poverty, Rachel's barrenness, Leah's tender eyes, the blindness of the man who had been so from his birth (John 9:1). Now, the crooks of this kind are of God's making, by the efficacy of his power directly bringing them to pass, and causing them to be. He is the maker of the poor, Proverbs 17:5: 'Whoso mocketh the poor, reproacheth his Maker'; that is, reproaches God who made him poor, according to that, 1 Samuel 2:7: 'The Lord maketh poor'. It is he that hath the key of the womb, and as he sees fit, shuts it (1 Sam. 1:5) or opens it (Gen. 29:31). And it is 'he that formeth the eyes' (Ps. 94:9). And the man was 'born blind, that the works of God should be made manifest in him' (John 9:3). Therefore he saith to Moses, Exodus 4:11: 'Who maketh the dumb, or deaf, or the seeing, or the blind? Have not I, the Lord?' Such crooks in the lot are of God's making, in the most ample sense, and in their full comprehension, being the direct effects of his agency, as well as the heavens and the earth.

There are impure sinful crooks, which, in their own nature, are sins as well as afflictions, defiling as well as grievous. Such was the crook made in David's lot, through his family disorders, the defiling of Tamar, the murder of Amnon, the rebellion of Absalom, all of them unnatural. Of the same kind was that made in Job's lot by the Sabeans and Chaldeans, taking away his substance and slaying his servants. As these were the afflictions of David and Job respectively, so they were the sins of the actors, the unhappy instruments thereof. Thus one and the same thing may be, to one a heinous sin, defiling and laying him under guilt, and to another an affliction, laying him under

35

suffering only. Now, the crooks of this kind are not of God's making, in the same latitude as those of the former: for he neither puts evil in the heart of any, nor stirreth up to it: 'He cannot be tempted with evil, neither tempteth he any man' (James 1:13). But they are of his making, by his holy permission of them, powerful bounding of them, and wise overruling of them to some good end.

He holily permits them, suffering men 'to walk in their own ways' (Acts 14:16). Though he is not the author of those sinful crooks, causing them to be, by the efficacy of his power: yet, if he did not permit them, willing not to hinder them, they could not be at all: for 'he shutteth and no man openeth' (Rev. 3:7). But he justly withholds his grace which the sinner does not desire, takes off the restraint under which he is uneasy, and since the sinner will be gone, lays the reins on his neck, and leaves him to the swing of his lust, 'Ephraim is joined to idols; let him alone' (Hosea 4:17). 'Israel would none of me: so I gave them up to their own heart's lusts' (Ps. 81:11, 12). In which unhappy situation the sinful crook doth, from the sinner's own proper motion, naturally and infallibly follow; even as water runs down a hill, wherever there is a gap left open before it. So in these circumstances, 'Israel walked in their own counsels' (v. 12). And thus this kind of crook is of God's making, as a just judge, punishing the sufferer by it. This view of the matter silenced David under Shimei's cursings, 2 Samuel 16:10, 11: 'Let him alone, and let him curse, for the Lord hath bidden him'.

He powerfully bounds them, Psalm 76:10: 'The remainder of wrath' (that is, the creature's wrath) 'thou shalt restrain'. Did not God bound these crooks, howsoever sore they are in any one's case, they would be yet sorer. But he says to the sinful instrument, as he said to the sea, 'Hitherto shalt thou come, but no farther; and here shall thy proud waves be stayed'. He lays a restraining band on him, that he cannot go one step farther, in the way his impetuous lust drives, than he sees meet to permit. Hence it comes to pass, that the crook of this kind is neither more nor less, but just as great as he by his powerful bounding makes it to be. An eminent instance hereof we have in the case of Job, whose lot was crooked through a peculiar agency of the devil; but even to that grand sinner, God set a bound in the case: 'The Lord said unto Satan, "Behold all that he hath is in thy power, only upon himself put not forth thy hand"' (Job 1:12). Now Satan went the full length of the bound, leaving nothing within the compass thereof untouched, which he saw could make for his purpose (vv. 18, 19). But he could by no means move one step beyond it, to carry his point, which he could not gain within it. And therefore, to make the trial greater, and the crook sorer, nothing remained but that the bound set should be removed, and the sphere of his agency enlarged; for which cause he says, 'But touch his bone and his flesh, and he will curse thee to thy face' (ch. 2:5). And it being removed accordingly, but withal a new one set (v. 6): 'Behold he is in thine hand, but save his life'; the crook was carried to the utmost that the new bound would permit, in a consistency with his design of bringing Job to blaspheme. 'Satan smote him with sore boils, from the sole of his foot unto the crown of his head' (v. 7). And had it not been for this bound, securing Job's life, he, after finding this attempt unsuccessful too, had doubtless despatched him at once.

He wisely overrules them to some good purpose, becoming the divine perfections. While the sinful instrument hath an ill design in the crook caused by him, God directs it to a holy and good end. In the disorders of David's family, Amnon's design was to gratify a brutish lust; Absalom's, to glut himself with revenge, and to satisfy his pride and ambition; but God meant thereby to punish David for his sin in the matter of Uriah. In the crook made in Job's lot, by Satan, and the Sabeans and Chaldeans, his instruments, Satan's design was to cause Job to blaspheme, and theirs to gratify their covetousness: but God had another design therein becoming himself, namely, to manifest Job's sincerity and uprightness. Did not he wisely and powerfully overrule these crooks made in men's lot, no good could come out of them; but he always overrules them so as to fulfil his own holy purposes thereby: (howbeit the sinner meaneth not so) for his designs cannot miscarry, his 'counsel shall stand' (Isa. 46:10). So the sinful crook is, by the overruling hand of God, turned about to his own glory, and his people's good in the end; according to the word, 'The Lord hath made all things for himself' (Prov. 16:4). 'All things work together for good to them that love God' (Rom. 8:28). Thus Haman's plot for the destruction of the Jews, 'was turned to the contrary' (Esther 9:1). And the crook made in Joseph's lot, by his own brethren selling him into Egypt, though it was on their part most sinful, and of a most mischievous design. Yet, as it was of God's making, by his holy permission, powerful bounding, and wisely overruling it, had an issue well becoming the divine wisdom and goodness: both of which Joseph notices to them, 'As for you, ye thought evil against me; but God meant it unto good, to bring to pass, as it is this day, to save much people alive' (Gen. 50:20).

God's Wisdom in Afflicting Man.

It remains to inquire, why God makes a crook in one's lot? And this is to be cleared by discovering the design of that dispensation: a matter that concerns everyone to know, and carefully to notice, in order to [gain] a Christian improvement of the crook in the lot. The design thereof seems to be chiefly, sevenfold.

A Test of True Faith.

The trial of one's state, whether one is in the state of grace or not? Whether a sincere Christian, or a hypocrite? Though every affliction is trying, yet here I conceive lies the main providential trial a man is brought into, with reference to his state; forasmuch as the crook in the lot, being a matter of a continued course, one has occasion to open and show himself again and again in the same thing; whence it comes to pass, that it ministers ground for a decision in that momentous point. It was plainly on this foundation that the trial of Job's state was put. The question was, whether Job was an upright and sincere servant of God, as God himself testified of him; or but a mercenary one, a hypocrite, as Satan alleged against him? And the trial hereof was put upon the crook to be made in his lot (Job 1:8-12; 2:3-6). Accordingly, that which all his friends, save Elihu, the last speaker, did, in their reasoning with him under his trial, aim at, was to prove him a hypocrite; Satan thus making use of these good men for gaining his point. As God made trial of Israel in the wilderness, for the land of Canaan, by a train of afflicting dispensations, which Caleb and Joshua bearing strenuously, were declared meet to enter the promised land, as having followed the Lord fully; while others being tired out with them, their carcasses fell in the wilderness; so he makes trial of men for heaven, by the crook in their lot. If one can stand that test, he is manifested to be a saint, a sincere servant of God, as Job was proved to be; if not, he is but a hypocrite: he cannot stand the test of the crook in his lot, but goes away like dross in God's furnace. A melancholy instance of which we have in that man of honour and wealth, who, with high pretences of religion, arising from a principle of moral seriousness, addressed himself to our Saviour, to know 'what he should do that he might inherit eternal life' (Mark 10:17-22). Our Saviour, to discover the man to himself, makes a crook in his lot, where all along before it had stood even, obliging him, by a probatory command, to sell and give away all that he had, and follow him (v. 21), 'Sell whatsoever thou hast and give to the poor, and come take up the cross and follow me'. Hereby he was, that moment, in the court of conscience, stripped of his great possessions; so that thenceforth he could no longer keep them, with a good conscience, as he might have done before. The man instantly felt the smart of this crook made in his lot: 'he was sad at that saying' (v. 22), that is, immediately upon the hearing of it, being struck with pain, disorder, and confusion of mind, his countenance changed, became cloudy and lowering, as the same word is used (Matt. 16:3). He could not stand the test of that crook; he could by no means submit his lot to God in that point, but behoved to have it, at any rate, according to his own mind. So he 'went away grieved, for he had great possessions'. He went away from Christ back to his plentiful estate, and though with a pained and sorrowful heart, sat him down again on it a violent possessor before the Lord, thwarting the divine order. And there was no appearance that ever this order was revoked, or that ever he came to a better temper in reference thereunto.

2

An Encouragement to Christian Duty

He is encouraged to duty, weaned one from this world, prompting him to look after the happiness of the other world. Many have been beholden to the crook in their lot, for that ever they came to themselves, settled, and turned serious. Going for a time like a wild ass used to the wilderness, scorning to be turned, their foot hath slid in due time; and a crook being thereby made in their lot, their month hath come wherein they have been caught (Jer. 2:24). Thus was the prodigal brought to himself, and obliged to entertain thoughts of returning unto his father (Luke 15:17). The crook in their lot convinces them at length that here is not their rest. Finding still a pricking thorn of uneasiness, whensoever they lay down their head where they would fain take rest in the creature, and that they are obliged to lift it again, they are brought to conclude, there is no hope from that quarter, and begin to cast about for rest another way, so it makes them errands to God, which they had not before; forasmuch as they feel a need of the comforts of the other world, to which their mouths were out of taste, while their lot stood even to their mind. Wherefore, whatever use we make of the crook in our lot, the voice of it is, 'Arise ye and depart, this is not your rest'. And it is surely that, which of all means of mortification, of the afflictive kind, doth most deaden a real Christian to this life and world.

Reproving Sin.

The Conviction of sin: as when one walking heedlessly is suddenly taken ill of a lameness: his going halting the rest of his way convinces him of having made a wrong step, and every new painful step brings it afresh to his mind. So God makes a crook in one's lot, to convince him of some false step he hath made, or course he hath taken. What the sinner would otherwise be apt to overlook, forget, or think light of, is by this means recalled to mind, set before him as an evil and bitter thing, and kept in remembrance, that his heart may every now and then bleed for it afresh. Thus, by the crook, men's sin finds them out to their conviction, 'as the thief is ashamed when he is found' (Num. 32:23; Jer. 2:26). The same Joseph's brethren feelingly expressed, under the crook made in their lot in Egypt, 'We are verily guilty concerning our brother' (Gen. 42:21). 'God hath found out the iniquity of thy servants' (ch. 44:16). The crook in the lot doth usually, in its nature or circumstances naturally refer to the false step or course that it serves for a providential memorial of it. Bringing the sin, though of an old date, fresh to remembrance, and for a badge of the sinner's folly, in word or deed, to keep it ever before him. When Jacob found Leah, through Laban's unfair deal-ing, palmed upon him for Rachel, how could he miss of a stinging remembrance of the cheat he had, seven years at least before, put on his own father, pretending himself to be Esau (Gen. 27:19)? How could it miss of galling him occasionally afterwards during the course of the marriage? He had imposed on his father the younger brother for the elder; and Laban imposed on him the elder sister for the younger. The dimness of Isaac's eyes favoured the former cheat; and the darkness of the evening did as much favour the latter. So he behoved to say, as Adoni-bezek in another case, (Judg. 1:7), 'As I have done, so God hath requited me'. In like manner, Rachel dying in childbirth, could hardly avoid a melancholy reflection on her rash and passionate expression, mentioned in Genesis 30:1, 'Give me children, or I die'. Even holy Job read, in the crook of his lot, some false steps he had made in his youth, many years before (Job 13:26), 'Thou writest bitter things against me, and makest me to possess the iniquities of my youth'.

Correction.

Correction, or punishment for sin. In nothing more than in the crook of the lot, is that word verified, 'Thine own wickedness shall correct thee, and thy backslidings shall reprove thee' (Jer. 2:19). God may, for a time, wink at one's sin, which afterward he will set a brand of his indignation upon, in crooking the sinner's lot, as he did in the case of Jacob, and of Rachel, mentioned before. Though the sin was a passing action, or a course of no long continuance, the mark of the divine displeasure for it, set on the sinner in the crook of his lot, may pain him long and sore, that by repeated experience he may know what an evil and bitter thing it was. David's killing Uriah by the sword of the Ammonites was soon over; but for that cause 'the sword never departed from his house' (2 Sam. 12:10). Gehazi quickly obtained two bags of money from Naaman, in the way of falsehood and lying; but as a lasting mark of the divine indignation against the profane trick, he got withal a leprosy which clave to him while he lived, and to his posterity after him (2 Kings 5:27). This may be the case, as well where the sin is pardoned, as to the guilt of eternal wrath, as where it is not. And one may have confessed and sincerely repented of that sin, which yet shall make him go halting to the grave, though it cannot carry him to hell. A man's person may be accepted in the Beloved, who yet hath a particular badge of the divine displeasure, with his sin hung upon him in the crook of his lot 'Thou wast a God that forgavest them, though thou tookest vengeance on their inventions' (Ps. 99:8).

Preventing Sin.

Preventing of sin. 'I will hedge up thy way with thorns, and make a wall that she shall not find her paths' (Hosea 2:6). The crook in the lot will readily be found to lie cross to some wrong bias of the heart, which peculiarly sways with the party: so it is like a thorn-hedge or wall in the way which the bias inclines him to. The defiling objects in the world do specially take and prove ensnaring, as they are suited to the particular cast of temper in men: but by means of the crook in the lot, the paint and varnish is worn off the defiling object, whereby it loses its former taking appearance: thus, the edge of corrupt affections is blunted, temptation weakened, and much sin prevented; the sinner after 'gadding about so much to change his way, returning ashamed' (Jer. 2:36, 37). Thus the Lord crooks one's lot that 'he may withdraw man from his purpose, and hide pride from men': and so 'he keepeth back his soul from the pit'

44

(Job 33:17, 18). Every one knows what is most pleasant to him; but God alone knows what is most profitable. As all men are liars, so all men are fools too: He is the only wise God (Jude 25). Many are obliged to the crook in their lot, that they go not to those excesses, which their vain minds and corrupt affections would with full sail carry them to; and they would from their hearts bless God for making it, if they did but calmly consider what would most likely be the issue of the removal thereof. When one is in hazard of fretting under the hardship of bearing the crook, he would do well to consider what condition he is as yet in to bear its removal in a Christian manner.

Discovery of Corruption.

Discovery of latent corruption, whether in saints or sinners. There are some corruptions in every man's heart, which lie, as it were, so near the surface, that they are ready on every turn to rise up; but then there are others also which lie so very deep, that they are scarcely observed at all. But as the fire under the pot makes the scum to rise up, appear a-top and run over; so the crook in the lot raises up from the bottom, and brings out, such corruptions as otherwise one could hardly imagine to be within. Who would have suspected such strength of passion in the meek Moses as he discovered at the waters of strife, and for which he was kept out of Canaan? (Ps. 106:32, 33; Num. 20:13). So much bitterness of spirit in the patient Job, as to charge God with becoming cruel to him? (Job 30:21). So much ill-nature in the good Jeremiah, as to curse not only the day of his birth, but even the man who brought tidings of it to his father? (Jer. 20:14, 15). Or, such a tang of atheism in Asaph, as to pronounce religion a vain thing? (Ps. 73:13).

45

But the crook in the lot, bringing out these things, showed them to have been within, [despite] how long they had lurked unobserved. And as this design, however indecently proud scoffers allow themselves to treat it, is in no way inconsistent with the divine perfections; so the discovery itself is necessary for the due humiliation of sinners, and to stain the pride of all glory, that men may know themselves. Both which appear, in that it was on this very design that God made the long-continued crook in Israel's lot in the wilderness; even to humble them and prove them, to know what was in their heart (Deut. 8:2).

The Grace of God.

The exercise of grace in the children of God. Believers, through the remains of indwelling corruption, are liable to fits of spiritual laziness and inactivity, in which their graces lie dormant for the time. Besides, there are some graces, which of their own nature are but occasional in their exercise; as being exercised only upon occasion of certain things which they have a necessary relation to: such as patience and long-suffering. Now, the crook in the lot serves to rouse up a Christian to the exercise of the graces, overpowerd by corruption, and withal to call forth to action the occasional graces, ministering proper occasions for them. The truth is, the crook in the lot is the great engine of Providence for making men appear in their true colours, discovering both their ill and their good; and if the grace of God be in them, it will bring it out, and cause it to display itself. It so puts the Christian to his shifts, that however it makes him stagger for awhile, yet it will at length evidence both the reality and the strength of grace in him. 'Ye are in heaviness through manifold temptations, that the trial of your faith, being much more precious than of gold that perisheth, may be found unto praise' (1 Pet. 1:6, 7). The crook in the lot gives rise to many acts of faith, hope, love, self-denial, resignation, and other graces; to many heavenly breathings, pantings, and groanings, which otherwise would not be brought forth. And I make no question but these things, however by carnal men despised as trifling, are more precious in the sight of God than even believers themselves are aware of, being acts of immediate internal worship; and will have a surprising notice taken of them, and of the sum of them, at long run, howbeit the persons themselves often can hardly think them worth their own notice at all. The steady acting of a gallant army of horse and foot to the routing of the enemy, is highly prized; but the acting of holy fear and humble hope, is in reality far more valuable, as being so in the sight of God, whose judgment, we are sure, is according to truth. This the Psalmist teaches, 'He delighteth not in the strength of the horse; he taketh not pleasure in the legs of a man. The Lord taketh pleasure in them that fear him, in those that hope in his mercy' (Ps. 147:10, 11). And indeed the exercise of the graces of his Spirit in his people, is so very precious in his sight, that whatever grace any of them excel in, they will readily get such a crook made in their lot as will be a special trial of it, that will make a proof of its full strength. Abraham excelled in the grace of faith, in trusting God's bare word of promise above the dictates of sense: and God, giving him a promise, that he would make of him a great nation, made withal a crook in his lot, by which he had enough ado with all the strength of his faith; while he was obliged to leave his country and kindred, and sojourn among the Canaanites; his wife continuing barren, till past the age of child-bearing: and when she had at length brought forth Isaac, and he was grown up, he was called to offer him up for a burnt-offering, the more exquisite trial of his faith, that Ishmael was now expelled his family, and that it was declared, that in Isaac only his seed should be called (Gen. 21:12). 'Moses was very meek above all the men which were upon the face of the earth' (Num. 12:3). And he was entrusted with the conduct of a most perverse and unmanageable people, the crook in his lot plainly designed for the exercise of his meekness. Job excelled in patience, and by the crook in his lot, he got as much to do with it. For God gives none of his people to excel in a gift, but some time or other he will afford them use for the whole compass of it.

Now, the use [application] of this doctrine is threefold. (1) For reproof. (2) For consolation. And (3) For exhortation.

1. *For reproof*: and it meets with three sorts of persons as reprovable.

First, the carnal and earthly, who do not with awe and reverence regard the crook in their lot as of God's making. There is certainly a signature of the divine hand upon it to be perceived by just observers; and that challenges an awful regard, the neglect of which forebodes destruction. 'Because they regard not the works of the Lord, nor the operation of his hands, he shall destroy them, and not build them up' (Ps. 28:5). And herein they are deeply guilty, who, poring upon second causes, and looking no further than the unhappy instruments of the crook in their lot, overlook the first cause, as a dog snarls at the stone, but looks not to the hand that casts it. This is, in effect, to make a God of the creature; so regarding it, as if it could of itself effect any thing, while, in the mean time, it is but an instrument in the hand of God, 'the rod of his anger' (Isa. 10:5). 'Ordained of him for judgment, established for correction' (Hab. 1:12). O! why should men terminate their view on the instruments of the crook in their lot, and so magnify their scourges? The truth is, they are, for the most part, rather to be pitied, as having an undesirable office, which for their gratifying their own corrupt affections, in making the crook in the lot of others, returns on their own head at length with a vengeance, as did 'the blood of Jezreel on the house of Jehu' (Hosea 1:4). And it is specially undesirable to be so employed in the case of such as belong to God; for rarely is the ground of the quarrel the same on the part of the instrument as on God's part, but very different; witness Shimei's cursing David, as a bloody man, meaning the blood of the house of Saul, which he was not guilty of, while God meant it of the blood of Uriah, which he could not deny (2 Sam. 16:7, 8). Moreover, the quarrel will be, at length, taken up between God and his people. And then their scourgers will find they had but a thankless office (Zech. 1:15), 'I was but a little displeased, and they helped forward the affliction,' says God, in resentment of the heathen crooking the lot of his people. In like manner are they guilty, who impute the crook in their lot to fortune, or their ill-luck, which in very deed is nothing but a creature of imagination, framed for a blind to keep man from acknowledging the hand of God. Thus, what the Philistines doubted, they do more impiously determine, saying, in effect, 'It is not his hand that smote us, it was a chance that happened to us' (1 Sam. 6:9). And, finally, those also are guilty, who, in the way of giving up themselves to carnal mirth and sensuality, set themselves to despise the crook in their lot, to make nothing of it, and to forget it. I question not, but one

49

committing his case to the Lord, and looking to him for remedy in the first place, may lawfully call in the moderate use of the comforts of life, for help in the second place. But as for that course so frequent and usual in this case among carnal men, if the crook of the lot really be, as indeed it is, of God's making, it must needs be a most indecent unbecoming course, to be abhorred of all good men. 'My son, despise not the chastening of the Lord' (Prov. 3:11). It is surely a very desperate measure of cure, which cannot miss of issuing in something worse than the disease, however it may palliate it for a while, 'In that day did the Lord God of hosts call to weeping and to mourning, and behold joy and gladness, eating flesh and drinking wine: and it was revealed in mine ears, by the Lord of hosts, Surely this iniquity shall not be purged from you till ye die' (Isa. 22:12-14).

The unsubmissive, whose hearts, like the troubled sea, swell and boil, fret and murmur, and cannot be at rest under the crook in their lot. This is a most sinful and dangerous course. The apostle Jude, characterising some, 'to whom is reserved the blackness of darkness for ever' (v. 13) says of them (v. 16), 'These are murmurers, complainers', namely, still complaining of their lot, which is the import of the word there used by the Holy Ghost. For, since the crook in their lot, which their unsubdued spirits can by no means submit to, is of God's making, this their practice must needs be a fighting against God: and these their complaining and murmuring are indeed against him, whatever face they put upon them. Thus when the Israelites murmur against Moses (Num.14:2), God charges them with murmuring against himself: 'How long shall I bear with this evil congregation, which murmured against me?' (v. 27). Ah! May not He who made and fashioned us without our advice, be allowed to make our lot too, without asking our mind, but we must rise up against him on account of the crook made in it? What doth this speak, but that the proud creature cannot endure God's work, nor bear what he hath done? And how black and dangerous is that temper of spirit! How is it possible to miss of being broken to pieces in such a course? 'He is wise in heart, and mighty in strength: who hath hardened himself against him and hath prospered?' (Job 9:4).

The careless and unfruitful do not set themselves dutifully to comply with the design of the crook in their lot. God and nature do nothing in vain. Since he makes the crook, there is, doubtless, a becoming design in it, which we are obliged in duty to fall in with, according to that, (Micah 6:9), 'Hear ye the rod'. And, indeed, if one shut not his own eyes, but be willing to understand, he may easily perceive the general design thereof to be, to wean him from this world, and move him to seek and take up his heart's rest in God. And nature and the circumstances of the crook itself being duly considered, it will not be very hard to make a more particular discovery of the design thereof. But, alas! The careless sinner, sunk in spiritual sloth and stupidity, is in no concern to discover the design of Providence in the crook; so he cannot fall in with it, but remains unfruitful; and all the pains taken on him, by the great Husbandman, in the dispensation, are lost. 'They cry out by reason of the arm of the mighty'; groaning under the pressure of the crook itself, and weight of the hand of the instrument thereof: 'But none saith, Where is God my Maker?' they look not, they turn not unto God for all that (Job 35:9, 10).

2. *For consolation*: it speaks comfort to the afflicted children of God. Whatever is the crook in your lot, it is of God's

51

making; and therefore you may look upon it kindly. Since it is your Father has made it for you, question not but there is a favourable design in it towards you. A discreet child welcomes his father's rod, knowing that being a father, he seeks his benefit thereby; and shall not God's children welcome the crook in their lot, as designed by their Father, who cannot mistake his measures, to work for their good, according to the promise? The truth is, the crook in the lot of a believer, however painful it proves, is a part of the discipline of the covenant, the nurture secured to Christ's children, by the promise of the Father, 'If his children forsake my law, and walk not in my judgments, then will I visit their transgressions with the rod' (Ps. 89:30, 32). Furthermore, all who are disposed to betake themselves to God under the crook in their lot, may take comfort in this, let them know that there is no crook in their lot but may be made straight; for God made it, surely then he can mend it. He himself can make straight what he hath made crooked, though none other can. There is nothing too hard for him to do: 'He raiseth up the poor out of the dust, and lifteth the needy out of the dunghill; that he may set him with princes. He maketh the barren woman to keep house and to be a joyful mother of children' (Ps. 113:7-9). Say not that your crook has been so long continued, that it will never mend. Put it in the hand of God, who made it, that he may mend it, and wait on him: and if it be for your good, that it should be mended, it shall be mended; for 'no good thing will he withhold from them that walk uprightly' (Ps. 134:11).

3. *For exhortation*: since the crook in the lot is of God's making, then, eyeing [considering] the hand of God in

yours, be reconciled to it, and submit under it whatever it is. I say, eyeing [considering] the hand of God in it, for otherwise your submission under the crook in your lot cannot be a Christian submission, acceptable to God, having no reference to him as your party in the matter.

Objection I: But some will say, 'The crook in my lot is from the hand of the creature; and such a one too as I deserved no such treatment from.'

Answer: From what hath been already said, it appears that, although the crook in thy lot be indeed immediately from the creature's hand, yet it is mediately from the hand of God; there being nothing of that kind, no penal evil, but the Lord hath done it. Therefore, without all peradventure, God himself is the principal party, whoever be the less principal. And albeit thou hast not deserved thy crook at the hand of the instrument which he makes use of for thy correction, thou certainly deservest it at his hand; and he may make use of it immediately by himself, even as seems good in his sight.

Objection II: 'But the crook in my lot might quickly be evened, if the instrument or instruments thereof pleased; only there is no dealing with them, so as to convince them of their fault in making it.'

Answer: If it is so, be sure God's time is not as yet come, that the crook should be made even; for, if it were come, though they stand now like an impregnable fort, they would give way like a sandy bank under one's feet: 'they should bow down to thee with their face toward the earth, and lick up the dust of thy feet' (Isa. 49:23). Meanwhile, that state of the matter is so far from justifying one's not eyeing the hand of God in the crook in the lot, that it makes a piece of trial in which his hand very eminently appears, namely, that men should be signally injurious and burdensome to others, yet by no means susceptible of conviction. This was the trial of the church from her adversaries, 'All that found them have devoured them; and their adversaries said, We offend not: because they have sinned against the Lord, the habitation of justice' (Jer. 1:7). They were very abusive, and gave her barbarous usage; yet would they own no fault in the matter. How could they ward off the conviction? Were they verily blameless in their devouring the Lord's straying sheep? No, surely, they were not. Did they look upon themselves as ministers of the divine justice against her? No, they did not.

Some indeed would make a question here, 'How the adversaries of the church could celebrate her God as the habitation of justice?' But the original pointing of the text being retained, it appears, that there is no ground at all for this question here, and withal the whole matter is set in a clear light. 'All that found them have devoured them; and their adversaries said, We offend not: because they have sinned against the Lord, the habitation of justice.' These last are not the words of the adversaries, but the words of the prophet showing how it came to pass that the adversaries devoured the Lord's sheep, as they lighted on them, and withal stood to the defence of it, when they had done, far from acknowledging any wrong: the matter lay here, the sheep had sinned against the Lord, the habitation of justice; and, as a just punishment hereof from his hand, they could have no justice at the hand of their adversaries.

Wherefore, laying aside these frivolous pretences, and eyeing the hand of God, as that which hath bowed your lot in that part, and keeps it in the bow, be reconciled to, and submit under the crook, whatever it is, saying from the

54

heart, 'Truly this is a grief, and I must bear it' (Jer. 10:19). And to move you hereunto, consider:

1. It is a duty you owe to God, as your sovereign Lord and Benefactor. His sovereignty challenges our submission; and it can in no case be meanness of spirit to submit to the crook which his hand hath made in our lot, and to go quietly under the yoke that he hath laid on; but it is really madness for the potsherds of the earth, by their turbulent and refractory carriage under it, to strive with their Maker. And his beneficence to us, ill-deserving creatures, may well stop our mouth from complaining of his making a crook in our lot, who would have done us no wrong had he made the whole of it crooked: 'Shall we receive good at the hand of God, and shall we not receive evil?' (Job 2:10).

2. It is an unalterable statute, for the time of this life, that nobody shall want a crook in their lot: for 'man is born unto trouble as the sparks fly upward' (Job 5:7). And those who are designed for heaven, are in a special manner assured of a crook in theirs, 'that in the world they shall have tribulation' (John 16:33); for by means thereof the Lord makes them meet for heaven. And how can you imagine that you shall be exempted from the common lot of mankind? 'Shall the rock be removed out of his place for thee?' And since God makes the crooks in men's lot according to the different exigence of their cases, you may be sure that yours is necessary for you.

3. A crook in the lot, which one can by no means submit to, makes a condition of all things like that in hell. For there a yoke, which the wretched sufferers can neither bear nor shake off, is wreathed about their necks; there the almighty arm draws against them, and they against it; there they are ever suffering and ever sinning; still in the

furnace, but their dross not consumed, nor they purified. Even such is the case of those who now cannot submit to the crook in their lot.

4. Great is the loss by not submitting to it. The crook in the lot, rightly improved, has turned to the best account, and made the best time to some that ever they had all their life long. As the Psalmist from his own experience testifies, 'Before I was afflicted, I went astray; but now have I kept thy word' (Ps. 119:67). There are many now in heaven, who are blessing God for the crook they had in their lot here. What a sad thing must it then be to lose this teeth-wind for Immanuel's land! But if the crook in thy lot do thee no good, be sure it will not miss of doing thee great damage; it will greatly increase your guilt and aggravate your condemnation, while it shall for ever cut thee to the heart, to think of the pains taken by means of the crook in the lot, to wean thee from the world, and bring you to God, but all in vain. Take heed, therefore, how you manage it, 'Lest - thou mourn at the last - and say, How have I hated instruction, and my heart despised reproof!' (Prov. 5:10-12).

Proposition II. What God sees meet to mar, we shall not be able to mend in our lot. What crook God makes in our lot, we shall not be able to even.

> **I. We shall show God's marring and making a crook in one's lot, as He sees meet.**
>
> **II. We shall consider men's attempting to mend or even that crook in their lot.**
>
> **III. In what sense it is to be understood, that we shall not be able to mend, or even the crook in our lot.**
>
> **IV. Render some reasons of the point.**

I. As to the first heading, namely, to show God's marring and making a crook in one's lot, as he sees meet.

God keeps the choice of every one's crook to himself; and therein he exerts his sovereignty (Matt. 20:15). It is not left to our option what that crook shall be, or what our peculiar burden; but, as the potter makes of the same clay one vessel for one use, another for another use, so God makes one crook for one, another for another, according to his own will and pleasure, 'Whatsoever the Lord pleased, that did he, in heaven and in earth' (Ps. 135:6).

He sees and observes the bias of every one's will and inclination, how it lies, and wherein it especially bends away from himself, and consequently wherein it needs the special bow. So he did in that man's case 'One thing thou lackest; go thy way, sell whatsoever thou hast, and give to the poor' (Mark 10:21). Observe the bent of his heart to his great possessions. He takes notice what is that idol that in every one's case is most apt to be his rival, that so he may suit the trial to the case, making the crook there.

By the conduct of his Providence, or a touch of his hand, he gives that part of one's lot a bow the contrary way; so that henceforth it lies quite contrary to the bias of the party's will (Ezek. 24:25). And here the trial is made, the bent of the will lying one way, and that part of one's lot another, that it does not answer the inclination of the party, but thwarts it.

He wills that crook in the lot to remain while he sees meet, for a longer or shorter time, just according to the holy ends he designs it for (2 Sam. 12:10; Hosea 5:15). By that will is so fixed, that the whole creation cannot alter it, or put it out of the bow.

II. We shall consider men's attempting to mend or even that crook in their lot.

This, in a word, lies in their making efforts to bring their lot in that point to their own will, that they may both go one way; so it imports three things:

A certain uneasiness under the crook in the lot; it is a yoke which is hard for the party to bear till his spirit be tamed and subdued (Jer. 31:18), 'Thou hast chastised me, and I was chastised, as a bullock unaccustomed to the yoke; turn thou me, and I shall be turned', etc. And it is for the breaking down of the weight of one's spirit that God lays it on: for which cause it is declared to be a good thing to bear it (Lam. 3:27), that being the way to make one at length as a weaned child.

A strong desire to have the cross removed, or to have matters in that part going according to our inclinations. This is very natural, nature desiring to be freed from every thing that is burdensome or cross to it; and if that desire be kept to a due subordination to the will of God, and it be not too peremptory, it is not sinful (Matt. 26:39), 'If it be possible, let this cup pass from me; nevertheless, not as I will', etc. Hence so many accepted prayers of the people of God, for the removal of the crook in their lot.

An earnest use of means for that end. This naturally follows on that desire. The man, being pressed with the cross, which is in his crook, labours all he can in the use of means to be rid of it. And if the means used be lawful, and not relied upon, but followed with an eye to God in them, the attempt is not sinful, whether he succeed in the use of them or not.

III. In what sense it is to be understood, that we shall not be able to mend or even the crook in our lot.

It is not to be understood, as if the case were absolutely hopeless, and that there is no remedy for the crook in the lot. For there is no case so desperate, but God may right it, 'Is anything too hard for the Lord?' (Gen. 18:14). When the crook has continued long, and spurned all remedies one has used for it, one is ready to lose hope about it; but many a crook, given over for hopeless that would never mend, God has made perfectly straight, as in Job's case.

But we shall never be able to mend it by ourselves; if the Lord himself take it not in hand to remove it, it will stand before us immovable, like a mountain of brass, though perhaps it may be in itself a thing that might easily be removed. We take it up in these three things:

1. It will never do by the mere force of our hand, 'For, by strength shall no man prevail' (1 Sam. 2:9). The most vigorous endeavours we can use will not even the crook, if God give it not a touch of his hand; so that all endeavours that way, without an eye to God, are vain and fruitless, and will be but ploughing on the rock (Ps. 127:1, 2).

2. The use of all allowable means for it, will be unsuccessful unless the Lord bless them for that end, 'Who is he that saith, and it cometh to pass, when the Lord commandeth it not?' (Lam. 3:37). As one may eat and not be satisfied, so one may use means proper for evening the crook in his lot, and yet prevail nothing. For nothing can be or do for us any more than God makes it to be or do (Eccles. 9:11), 'The race is not to the swift, nor the battle to the strong; neither yet bread to the wise, nor yet riches to men of understanding' etc.

3. It will never do in our time, but in God's time, which seldom is as early as ours, 'My time is not yet come, but

your time is always ready' (John 7:6). Hence that crook remains sometimes immovable, as if it were kept by an invisible hand; and at another time it goes away with a touch, because God's time is come for evening it.

IV. We shall now assign the reasons of the point.

Because of the absolute dependence we have upon God (Acts 17:28). As the light depends on the sun, or the shadow on the body, so we depend on God, and without him can do nothing, great or small. And God will have us to find it so, to teach us our dependence.

Because his will is irresistible (Isa. 46:10), 'My counsel shall stand, and I will do all my pleasure'. When God wills anything, and the creature the contrary, it is easy to see which will must be done. When the omnipotent arm holds, in vain does the creature draw, 'Who hath hardened himself against him and prospered?' (Job 9:4).

There is a necessity of yielding and submitting to the crook in our lot; for we may as well think to remove the rocks and mountains, which God has settled, as to make that part of our lot straight which he hath made crooked.

The evening of the crook in our lot, by main force of our own, is but a cheat we put on ourselves, and will not last, but, like a stick by main force made straight, it will quickly return to the bow again. The only effectual way of getting the crook evened, is to apply to God for it.

Exhortation: Let us then apply to God for removing any crook in our lot, that in the settled order of things may be removed. Men cannot cease to desire the removal of a crook, more than that of a thorn in the flesh. But, since we are not able to mend what God sees meet to mar, it is evident we are to apply to him that made it to amend it, and not take the evening of it in our own hand.

Motive: All our attempts for its removal will, without him, be vain and fruitless (Ps. 127:1). Let us be as resolute as we will to have it evened, if God say it not, we will labour in vain (Lam. 3:37). Howsoever fair the means we use bid for it, they will be ineffectual if he command not the blessing (Eccles. 9:11).

Such attempts will readily make it worse. Nothing is more ordinary, than for a proud spirit striving with the crook, to make it more crooked 'Whosoever breaketh a hedge, a serpent shall bite him. Whoso removeth stones, shall be hurt therewith' (Eccles. 10:8, 9). This is evident in the case of the murmurers in the wilderness. It naturally comes to be so; because, at that rate, the will of the party bends farther away from it: and, moreover, God is provoked to wreath the yoke faster about one's neck, that he will by no means let it sit easy on him.

There is no crook but what may be remedied by him, and made perfectly straight, 'The Lord raiseth them that are bowed down' (Ps. 146:8). He can perform that, concerning which there remains no hope with us, 'Who quickeneth the dead and calleth those things which be not as though they were?' (Rom. 4:17). It is his prerogative to do wonders; to begin a work, where the whole creation gives it over as hopeless, and carry it on to perfection (Gen. 18:14).

He loves to be employed in evening crooks, and calls us to employ him that way (Ps. 50:15), 'Call upon me in the day of trouble, and I will deliver thee' etc. He makes them for that very end, that he may bring us to him on that errand, and may manifest his power and goodness in evening of them (Hosea 5:15). The straits of the children of men afford a large field for displaying his glorious perfections, which otherwise would be wanting (Exod. 15:11).

A crook thus evened is a double mercy. There are some crooks evened by a touch of the hand of common providence, while people are either not exercised about them, or when they fret for their removal; these are sapless mercies, and short-lived (Ps. 78:30, 31; Hosea 13:11). Fruits thus too hastily plucked off the tree of providence can hardly miss to set the teeth on edge, and will certainly be bitter to the gracious soul. But O the sweets of the evening of the crook by a humble application to, and waiting on the Lord! It has the image and superscription of divine favour upon it, which makes it bulky and valuable (Gen. 33:10), 'For therefore I have seen thy face, as though I had seen the face of God' etc, (ch. 21:6).

God has signaled his favour to his dearest children, in making and mending notable crooks in their lot. His darling ones ordinarily have the greatest crooks made in their lot (Heb. 12:6). But then they make way for their richest experiences in the removal of them, upon their application to him. This is clear from the case of Abraham, Jacob, and Joseph. Which of the patriarchs had so great crooks as they? But which of them, on the other hand, had such signal tokens of the divine favour? The greatest of men, as Samson and John the Baptist, have been born of women naturally barren; so do the greatest crooks issue in the richest mercies to them that are exercised thereby.

It is the shortest and surest way to go straight to God with the crook in the lot. If we would have our wish in that point, we must, as the eagle, first soar aloft, and then come down on the prey. (Mark 5:36). Our faithless out-of-the-way attempts to even the crook, are but our fool's haste, that is no speed; as in the case of Abraham's going in to Hagar. God is the first mover, who sets all the wheels in motion for evening the crook, which without him will remain immovable (Hosea 2:21, 22).

Objection I: 'But it is needless, for I see, that though the crook in my lot may mend, yet it never will mend. In its own nature it is capable of being removed, but it is plain it is not to be removed, it is hopeless.'

Answer: That is the language of unbelieving haste, which faith and patience should correct (Ps. 116:11, 12). Abraham had as much to say for the hopelessness of his crook, but yet he applies to God in faith for the mending of it (Rom. 4:19, 20). Sarah had made such a conclusion, for which she was rebuked (Gen. 18:13, 14). Nothing can make it needless in such a case to apply to God.

Objection II: 'But I have applied to him again and again for it, yet it is never mended.'

Answer: Delays are not denials of suits at the court of heaven, but trials of faith and patience of the petitioners. And whoso will persevere will certainly speed at length (Luke 18:7, 8), 'And shall not God avenge his own elect, which cry day and night unto him, though he bear long with them? I tell you that he will avenge them speedily'. Sometimes indeed folks grow pettish, in the case of the crook in the lot, and let it drop out in their prayers, in a course of despondency, while yet it continues uneasy to them; but, if God mind to even it in mercy, he will oblige them to take it in again, 'I will yet, for this, be inquired of by the house of Israel, to do it for them' (Ezek. 36:37). If the removal come, while it is dropt, there will be little comfort in it: though it were never to be removed while we live, that should not cut off our applying to God for the removal; for there are many prayers not to be answered till we come to the other world (Rom. 7:24) and there all will be answered at once.

Directions for rightly managing the application for removing the crook in the lot.

1. Pray for it (Ezek. 36:37) and pray in faith, believing that, for the sake of Jesus, you shall certainly obtain at length, and in this life too, if it is good for you; but without peradventure in the life to come (Matt. 21:22). They will not be disappointed that get the song of Moses and of the Lamb (Rev. 15:3). And, in some cases of that nature, extraordinary prayer, with fasting, is very expedient (Matt. 17:21).

2. Humble yourselves under it, as the yoke which the sovereign hand has laid on you, 'I will bear the indignation of the Lord, because I have sinned against him'(Micah 7:9). Justify God, condemn yourselves, kiss the rod, and go quietly under it; this is the most feasible way to get rid of it, the end being obtained (James 4:10). 'Thou wilt prepare their hearts, thou wilt cause thine ear to hear' (Ps. 10:17).

3. Wait on patiently till the hand that made it mend it (Ps. 27:14). Do not give up the matter as hopeless, because you are not so soon relieved as you would wish; 'But let patience have her perfect work, that ye may be perfect and entire, wanting nothing' (James 1:4). Leave the timing of the deliverance to the Lord; his time will at length, to conviction, appear the best, and it will not go beyond it (Isa. 60:22), 'I, the Lord, will hasten it in his time'; waiting on him, you will not be disappointed, 'For they shall not be ashamed that wait for me' (Isa. 49:23).

Exhortation: What crook there is, which, in the settled order of things, cannot be removed or evened in this world, let us apply to God for suitable relief under it. For instance, the common crook in the lot of saints, viz in-dwelling sin; as God has made that crook not to be removed here, he can certainly balance it, and afford relief under it. The same is to be said of any crook, while it remains unremoved. In such cases apply yourself to God, for making up your losses another way. And there are five things I would have you to keep in view, and aim at here:

1. To take God in Christ for, and instead of that thing, the withholding or taking away of which from you makes the crook in your lot (Ps. 142:4, 5). There is never a crook which God makes in our lot, but it is in effect heaven's offer of a blessed exchange to us; such as Mark 10:21, 'Sell whatsoever thou hast, - and thou shalt have treasure in heaven'. In managing of which exchange, God first puts out his hand, and takes away some earthly thing from us; and it is expected we put out our hand next, and take some heavenly thing from him in the stead of it, and particularly his Christ. Wherefore has God emptied your left hand of such and such an earthly comfort? Stretch out your right hand to God in Christ, take him in the room of it and welcome. Therefore the soul's closing with Christ is called buying, wherein parting with one thing, we get another in its stead (Matt. 13:45, 46), 'The kingdom of heaven is like unto a merchantman seeking goodly pearls: who, when he had found one pearl of great price, he went and sold all that he had and bought it'. Do this, and you will be more than even hands with the crook in your lot.

2. Look for the stream running as full from him as ever it did or could run, when the crook of the lot has dried it. This is the work of faith, confidently to depend on God for that which is denied us from the creature. 'When my father and mother forsake me, then the Lord will take me up' (Ps. 27:10). This is a most rational expectation: for it is certain there is no good in the creature but what is from

God; therefore there is no good to be found in the creature, the stream, but what may be got immediately from God, the fountain. And it is a welcome plea, to come to God and say, 'Now, Lord, thou hast taken away from me such a creature-comfort, I must have as good from thyself.'

3. Seek for the spiritual fruits of the crook in the lot (Heb. 12:11). We see the way the world is, when one trade fails, to fall on and drive another trade; so should we, when there is a crook in the lot, making our earthly comforts low, set ourselves the more for spiritual attainments. If our trade with the world sinks, let us see to drive a trade with heaven more vigorously; see, if by means of the crook, we can obtain more faith, love, heavenly-mindedness, contempt of the world, humility, self-denial, etc (2 Cor. 6:10). So while we lose at one hand, we shall gain at another.

4. Grace to bear us up under the crook, 'For this thing I besought the Lord thrice'; and he said, 'My grace is sufficient for thee' (2 Cor. 12:8, 9). Whether a man be faint, and have a light burden, or be refreshed, and strengthened, and have a heavy one, it is all the same; the latter can go as easy under his burden as the former under his. Grace proportioned to the trial is what we should aim at; getting that, though the crook be not evened, we are even hands with it.

5. The keeping in our eye the eternal rest and weight of glory in the other world, 'For our light affliction, which is but for a moment, worketh for us a far more exceeding and eternal weight of glory; while we look not at the things which are seen, but at the things which are not seen' (2 Cor. 4:17, 18). This will balance the crook in your lot, be it what it will. While they who have no well-grounded hope of salvation, will find the crook in their lot in this world

such a weight, as they have nothing to counterbalance it; but the hope of eternal rest may bear up under all the toil and trouble met with here.

Exhortation: Let us then set ourselves rightly to bear the crook in our lot, while God sees meet to continue it. What we cannot mend, let us bear [in a] Christian [manner], and not fight against God, and so kick against the pricks.

Patience.

1. So let us bear it, patiently, without fuming and fretting, or murmuring (James 5:7; Ps. 37:7). Though we lose our comfort in the creature, through the crook in our lot, let us not lose the possession of ourselves (Luke 21:19). The crook in our lot makes us like one who has but a scanty fire to warm at: but impatience under it scatters it, so as to set the house on fire about us, and expose us to danger (Prov. 25:28), 'He that hath no rule over his own spirit, is like a city that is broken down, and without walls'.

Fortitude.

With Christian fortitude, without sinking under discouragement - 'nor faint when thou art rebuked of him' (Heb. 12:5). Satan's work is by the crook, either to bend or break people's spirits, and oftentimes by bending to break them: our work is to carry evenly under it, steering a middle course, guarding against splitting on the rocks on either hand. Our happiness lies not in any earthly comfort, nor will the want of any of them render us miserable (Hab. 3:17, 18). So that we are resolutely to hold on our way with a holy contempt, and regardless of hardships, 'The righteous also shall hold on his way, and he that hath clean hands shall be stronger and stronger' (Job 17:9).

Question: 'When may any one be reckoned to fall under sinking discouragement from the crook in his lot?'

Answer: When it prevails so far as to unfit us for the duties, either of our particular or Christian calling. We may be sure it has carried us beyond the bounds of moderate grief, when it unfits us for the common affairs of life, which the Lord calls us to manage (1 Cor. 7:24). Or for the duties of religion, hindering them altogether (1 Pet. 3:7), 'That your prayers be not hindered' (*Greek:* cut off, or cut up, like a tree from the roots), or making one quite hopeless in them (Mal. 2:13).

Profitably.

Let us bear it profitably, so as we may gain some advantage thereby (Ps. 119:71), 'It is good for me that I have been afflicted; that I might learn thy statutes'. There is an advantage to be made thereby (Rom. 5:3-5). And it is certainly an ill-managed crook in our lot, when we get not some spiritual good of it (Heb. 12:11). The crook is a kind of spiritual medicine; and as it is lost physic that purges away no ill humours, in vain are its unpleasantness to the taste and its gripings endured; so it is a lost crook, and ill is the bitterness of it borne if we are not bettered by it (Isa. 27:9), 'By this, therefore, shall the iniquity of Jacob be purged, and this is all the fruit, to take away his sin'.

Motives to press this exhortation.

1. There will be no evening of it while God sees meet to continue it. Let us behave under it as we will, and make what sallies we please in the case, it will continue immovable, as fixed with bands of iron and brass, 'But he is of one mind, and who can turn him? and what his soul desireth, even that he doth. For he performeth the thing

that is appointed for me; and many such things are with him' (Job 23:13, 14). Is it not wisdom then to make the best we may of what we cannot mend? Make a virtue then of necessity. What is not to be cured must be endured, and should with a Christian resignation.

2. An awkward carriage under it notably increases the pain of it. What makes the yoke gall our necks, but that we struggle so much against it, and cannot let it sit at ease on us (Jer. 31:18). How often are we, in that case, like men dashing their heads against a rock to remove it! The rock stands unmoved, but they are wounded, and lose exceedingly by their struggle. Impatience under the crook lays an over-weight on the burden, and makes it heavier, while withal it weakens us, and makes us less able to bear it.

3. The crook in thy lot is the special trial God has chosen for thee to take thy measure by (1 Pet. 1:6, 7). It is God's fire, whereby he tries what metal men are of; heaven's touchstone for discovering true and counterfeit Christians. They may bear, and go through several trials, whom the crook in the lot will discover to be naught, because, by no means they can bear that (Mark 10:21, 22). Think then with thyself under it; now, here the trial of my state turns; I must, by this, be proved either sincere, or a hypocrite; for, can any be a cordial subject of Christ, without being able to submit his lot to him? Do not all who sincerely come to Christ, put a blank in his hand? (Acts 9:6; Ps. 47:4). And does he not tell us, that without that disposition we are not his disciples? 'If any man come to me, and hate not his father and mother, and wife, and children, and brethren, and sisters, yea, and his own life also, he cannot be my disciple' (Luke 14:26). Perhaps you find you can submit to any thing but that; but will not that but mar all? (Mark 10:21, 22) Did ever any hear

of a sincere closing with Christ with a reserve or exception of one thing, wherein they chose to be their own lords?

Question: 'Is that disposition then a qualification necessarily pre-required to our believing: and if so, where must we have it? Can we work it out of our natural powers?'

Answer: No, it is not so; but it necessarily accompanies and goes along with believing, flowing from the same saving illumination in the knowledge of Christ, whereby the soul is brought to believe on him. Hereby the soul sees him an able Saviour, and so trusts on him for salvation; the rightful Lord and infinitely wise Ruler, and so submits the lot to him (Matt.13:45, 46). The soul taking him for a Saviour, takes him also for a head and ruler. It is Christ's giving himself to us, and our receiving him, that causes us to quit other things to and for him, as it is the light that dispels the darkness.

Case [illustration] 'Alas! I cannot get my heart freely to submit my lot to him in that point.'

Answer: That submission will not be carried on in any without a struggle. The old man will never submit to it, and when the new man of grace is submitting to it, the old man will still be rebelling, 'For the flesh lusteth against the spirit, and the spirit against the flesh. And these are contrary, the one to the other, so that ye cannot do the things that you would' (Gal. 5:17); but are ye sincerely desirous and habitually aiming to submit to it? From the ungracious struggle against the crook, turn away to the struggle with your own heart to bring it to submit, believing the promise and using the means for it, being grieved from the heart with yourself, that you cannot submit to it. This is submitting of your lot, in the favourable construction of the gospel (Rom. 7:17-20; 2 Cor. 8:12). If you had your choice, would you rather have your heart brought to submit to the crook, than the crook evened to your heart's desire? (Rom. 7:22, 23). And do you not sincerely endeavour to submit, notwithstanding the reluctance of the flesh (Gal. 5:17).

Where is the Christian self-denial, and taking up the cross, without submitting to the crook? This is the first lesson Christ puts in the hands of his disciples (Matt. 16:24), 'If any man will come after me, let him deny himself, and take up his cross, and follow me'. Self-denial would procure a reconciliation with the crook, and an admittance of the cross: but while we cannot bear our corrupt self to be denied any of its cravings, and particularly that which God sees meet especially to be denied, we cannot bear the crook in our lot, but fight against it in favour of self.

Where is our conformity to Christ, while we cannot submit to the crook? We cannot evidence ourselves Christians, without conformity to Christ. 'He that saith he abideth in him, ought himself also so to walk, even as he walked' (1 John 2:6). There was a continued crook in Christ's lot, but he submitted to it, 'And being found in fashion as a man, he humbled himself, and became obedient unto death, even the death of the cross' (Phil. 2:8). (Rom. 15:3). For even Christ pleased not himself etc. And so must we, if we will prove ourselves Christians indeed (Matt. 11:29; 2 Tim. 2:11, 12).

How shall we prove ourselves the genuine kindly children of God, if still warring with the crook? We cannot pray, Our Father, Thy will be done on earth, as, etc (Matt. 6). Nay, the language of that practice is, we must have our own will and God's will, cannot satisfy us.

4. The trial by the crook here will not last long (1 Cor. 7:29-31). What though the work be sore, it may

be the better comported with, that it will not be longsome; a few days or years at farthest, will put an end to it, and take you off your trials. Do not say, I shall never be eased of it; for if not eased before, you will be eased of it at death, come after it what will. A serious view of death and eternity might make us set ourselves to behave rightly under our crook while it lasts.

5. If you would, in a Christian manner, set yourselves to bear the crook, you would find it easier than you imagine, 'Take my yoke upon you, and learn of me, and ye shall find rest to your souls; for my yoke is easy, and my burden is light' (Matt. 11:29, 30). Satan has no readier way to gain his purpose, than to persuade men it is impossible that ever their minds should ply with the crook; that it is a burden to them, altogether insupportable; as long as you believe that, be sure you will never be able to bear it. But the Lord makes no crook in the lot of any, but what may be borne of them acceptably, though not sinlessly and perfectly (Matt. 11:30). For there is strength for that effect secured in the covenant (2 Cor. 3:5; Phil. 4:13) and being by faith fetched, it will certainly come (Ps. 28:7).

6. If you behave [in a] Christian [manner] under your crook here, you will not lose your labour, but get a full reward of grace in the other world, through Christ (2 Tim. 2:12; 1 Cor. 15:58). There is a blessing pronounced on him that endureth on this very ground (James 1:12), 'Blessed is the man that endureth temptation; for, when he is tried, he shall receive the crown of life which the Lord hath promised to them that love him'. Heaven is the place into which the approved, upon the trial of the crook, are received (Rev. 7:14), 'These are they which came out of great tribulation, and have washed their robes, and made them

white in the blood of the Lamb'. When you come there, no vestiges of it will be remaining in your lot, nor will you have the least uneasy remembrance of it; but it will accent your praises, and increase your joy.

7. If you do not behave [in a] Christian [manner] under it, you will lose your souls in the other world (Jude 15, 16). Those who are at war with God in their lot here, God will have war with them forever. If they will not submit to his yoke here, and go quietly under it, he will wreathe his yoke about their neck forever, with everlasting bonds that shall never be loosed (Job 9:4). Therefore, set yourselves to behave rightly under the crook in your lot.

If you ask what way one may reach that; for direction we propose:

Proposition III. The considering the crook in the lot, as the work of God, is a proper means to bring one to behave rightly under it.

I. What it is to consider the crook as the work of God. We take it up in these five things:

An inquiry into the spring whence it rises (Gen. 25:22). Reason and religion both teach us, not only to notice the crook, which we cannot avoid, but to consider and inquire into the spring of it. Surely, it is not our choice, nor do we designedly make it for ourselves: and to ascribe it to fortune is to ascribe it to nothing: it is not sprung of itself, but sown by one hand or another for us (Job 5:6). And we are to notice the hand from whence it comes.

The hand of God is perceived in it. Whatever hand any creatures have therein, we ought not to terminate our view in them, but look above and beyond them to the supreme manager's agency (Job 1:21). Without this we shall make a God of the creature that is instrumental of the crook. Looking on it as if it were the first cause, which is peculiar to God (Rom. 11:36), and bring ourselves under that doom, 'Because they regard not the works of the Lord, nor the operation of his hands, he shall destroy them, and not build them up' (Ps. 28:5).

Representing it to ourselves as a work of God, which he hath wrought against us for holy and wise ends, becoming the divine perfections. This is to take it by the right handle, to represent it to ourselves, under a right notion, from whence a right management under it may spring. It can never be safe to overlook God in it, but very safe to overlook the creature; ascribing it unto God, as if no other hand were in it, his being always the principal therein. 'It is the Lord, let him do what seemeth him good' (1 Sam. 3:18). Thus David overlooked Shimei, and looked to God in the matter of his cursing, as one fixing his eyes, not on the axe, but on him that wielded it. Here two things are to come into our consideration.

The decree of God, purposing that crook for us from eternity; 'for he worketh all things after the counsel of his own will' (Eph. 1:11), the sealed book, in which are written all the black lines that make the crook. Whatever valleys of darkness, grief, and sorrow, we are carried through, we are to look on them as made by the mountains of brass, the immovable divine purposes (Zech. 6:1). This can be no presumption in that case, if we carry it no further than the event goes in our sight and feeling: for so far the book is opened for us to look into.

The Providence of God bringing to pass that crook for us in time (Amos 3:6). There is nothing can befall us without him in whom we live. Whatever kind of agency of the creatures may be in the making of our crook, whatever they have done or not done towards it, he is the spring that sets all the created wheels in motion, which ceasing, they would all stop: though he is still infinitely pure in his agency, however impure they be in theirs. Job considered both these (ch. 23:14).

A continuing in the thought of the crook as such. It is not a simple glance of the eye, but a contemplating and leisurely viewing of it as his work, that is the proper mean.

We are to be, habitually impressed with this consideration: as the crook is some lasting grievance, so the consideration of this as the remedy should be habitually kept up. There are other considerations besides this that we must entertain, so that we cannot always have it expressly in our mind: but we must lay it down for a rooted principle, according to which we are to manage the crook, and keep the heart in a disposition, whereby it may expressly slip into our minds, as occasion calls.

We are to be occasionally exercised in it. Whenever we begin to feel the smart of the crook, we should fetch in this remedy; when the yoke begins to gall the back, there should be an application of this spiritual ointment. And however often the former comes in on us, it will be our wisdom to fetch in the latter as the proper remedy; the oftener it is used, it will more easily come to hand, and also be the more effectual.

A considering it for the end for which it is proposed to us, namely, to bring us to a dutiful carriage under it. Men's corruptions will cause them to enter on the consideration of it: but as the principle is, so the end and effect of it will be corrupt (2 Kings 6:33). But we must enter on, and use it for a good end, if we would profit from it, taking it as a practical consideration for regulating our conduct under the crook.

II. How it is to be understood to be a proper means to bring one to behave rightly under the crook.

Not as if it were sufficient of itself, and as it stands alone, to produce that effect. But as it is used in faith, in the faith of the gospel; that is to say, A sinner's bare considering the crook in his lot as the work of God, without any saving relation to him, will never be a way to behave himself rightly under it: but having believed in Jesus Christ, and so taking God for his God, the considering of the crook as the work of God, his God, is the proper means to bring him to that desirable temper and behaviour. Many hearers mistake here. When they hear such and such lawful considerations proposed for bringing them to duty, they presently imagine, that by the mere force of them, they may gain the point. And many preachers too, who, forgetting Christ and the gospel, pretend by the force of reason to make men Christians. The eyes of both being held, that they do not see the corruption of men's nature, which is such as sets the true cure above the force of reason. All that they are sensible of, being some ill habits, which they think may be shaken off by a vigorous application of their rational faculties. To clear this matter, consider [the following]:

3

God Blesses His People Through Affliction

Is it rational to think to set fallen man, with his corrupted nature, to work the same way with innocent Adam? That is to set beggars on a level with the rich, lame men to a journey with those that have limbs. Innocent Adam had a stock of gracious abilities, whereby he might, by the force of moral considerations, have brought himself to perform duty aright. But where is that with us? (2 Cor. 3:5). Whatever force be in them to a soul endowed with spiritual life, what power have they to raise the dead, such as we are? (Eph. 2:1).

The scripture is very plain on this head, showing the indispensable necessity of faith (Heb. 11), and that, such as unites to Christ, 'Without me', that is, separate from me, 'ye can do nothing' (John 15:5); no, not with all the moral considerations you can use. How were the Ten Commandments given on mount Sinai? Not as a bare exaction of duty, but fronted with the gospel, to be believed in the first place; 'I am the Lord thy God' etc. And so Solomon, whom many regard rather as a moral philosopher, than an inspired writer leading to Christ, fronts his writings, in the beginning of the Proverbs, with most express gospel. And must we have it expressly repeated in our Bibles with every moral precept, or else shut our eyes and take these precepts without it? That is the effect of our natural enmity to Christ. If we loved him more, we should see him more in every page, and in every command, receiving the law at his mouth.

Do but consider what it is to behave rightly under the crook in the lot; what humiliation of soul, self-denial, and absolute resignation to the will of God must be in it. What love to God it must proceed from; how regard to his glory must influence it as the chief end thereof; and try, and see if it is not impossible for you to reach it without that faith aforementioned. I know a Christian may reach it without full assurance: but still, according to the measure of their persuasion that God is their God, so will their attainments in it be; these keep equal pace. O what kind of hearts do they imagine themselves to have, that think they can for a moment empty them of the creature, farther than they can fill them with a God, as their God, in its room and stead! No doubt men may, from the force of moral considerations, work themselves to behave under the crook, externally right, such as many pagans do; but a Christian disposition of spirit under it will never be reached, without that faith in God.

Objection: 'Then it is saints only that are capable of the improvement of that consideration.'

Answer: Yea, indeed it is so, as to that and all other moral considerations, for true Christian ends. And that amounts to no more, than that directions for walking rightly are only for the living, that have the use of their limbs: and, therefore, that you may improve it, set yourselves to believe in the first place.

I shall confirm that it is a proper mean to bring one to behave rightly under it. This will appear, if we consider these four things:

1. It is of great use to divert from the considering and dwelling on those things about the crook, which serve to irritate our corruption. Such are the balking of our will and wishes, the satisfaction we should have in the matter's going according to our mind, the instruments of the crook, how injurious they are to us, how unreasonable, how obstinate, etc. The dwelling on these considerations is but the blowing of the fire within. But to turn our eyes to it as the work of God, would be a cure by way of diversion (2 Sam. 6:9, 10); and such diversion of the thoughts is not only lawful, but expedient and necessary.

2. It has a moral aptitude for producing this good effect. Though our cure is not compassed by the mere force of reason; yet it is carried on, not by a brutal movement, but in a rational way (Eph. 5:14). This consideration has a moral efficacy on our reason, it is fit to awe us into a submission, and ministers a deal of argument for behaving [as a] Christian under our crook.

3. It has a divine appointment for that end, which is to be believed (Prov. 3:6). So the text. The creature in itself is an inefficacious and motionless thing, a mere vanity (Acts 17:28). That which makes any thing a means fit for the end, is a word of divine appointment (Matt. 4:4). To use any thing then for an end, without the faith of this, is to make a god of the creature; therefore it is to be used in a dependence on God, according to that word of appointment (1 Tim. 4:4, 5). And every thing is fit for the end for which God has appointed it. This consideration is appointed for that end; and therefore is a fit means for it.

4. The Spirit may be expected to work by it, and does work by it, in them that believe, and look to him for it, forasmuch as it is a mean of his own appointment. Papists, legalists, and all superstitious persons, devise various means of sanctification, seeming to have, or really having, a moral fitness for the same. But they are quite ineffectual, because, like Abana and Pharpar[1], they want a word of divine appointment for curing us of our leprosy. Therefore the Spirit works not by them, since they are not his instruments, but devised of their own hearts. And since even the means of divine appointment are ineffectual without the Spirit, these can never be effectual. But this consideration having a divine appointment, the Spirit works by it.

Use [application]: Then take this direction for your behaving rightly under the crook in your lot. Inure yourselves to consider it as the work of God. And for helping you to improve it, so as it may be effectual, I offer this advice:

1. Consider it as the work of your God in Christ. This is the way to sprinkle it with gospel-grace, and so to make it tolerable (Ps. 22:1). The discerning of a Father's hand in the crook will take out much of the bitterness of it, and sugar the pill to you. For this cause it will be necessary, (1) Solemnly to take God for your God, under your crook (Ps. 142:4, 5). (2) In all your encounters with it, resolutely to believe, and claim your interest in him (1 Sam. 30:6).

2. Enlarge the consideration with a view of the divine relations to you, and the divine attributes. Consider it, being the work of your God, the work of your Father, elder

---

1   The rivers of Damascus to which Naaman referred when he was commanded to cleanse himself in the river Jordan; 2 Kings 5:12; Ed.

Brother, Head, Husband, etc, who, therefore, surely consults your good. Consider his holiness and justice, showing he wrongs you not; his mercy and goodness, that it is not worse; his sovereignty, that may silence you: his infinite wisdom and love, that may satisfy you in it.

3. Consider what a work of his it is, how it is a convincing work, for bringing sin to remembrance; a correcting work, to chastise you for your follies; a preventing work, to hedge you up from courses of sin you would otherwise be apt to run into; a trying work, to discover your state, your graces, and corruption; a weaning work, to wean you from the world and fit you for heaven.

4. In all your considerations of it in this manner, look upward for his Spirit, to render them effectual (1 Cor. 3:6). Thus may you behave [in a] Christian [manner] under it, till God makes it even either here or in heaven.

> Better it is to be of an humble spirit with the lowly, than
> to divide the spoil with the proud (Prov. 16:9).

Could men once be brought to believe, that it is better to have their minds bend to the crook in their lot, than to force the crook to their mind, they would be in a fair way to bring their matters to a good account. Hear then the divine decision in that case: 'Better it is to be of an humble spirit with the lowly, than to divide the spoil with the proud'.

Humility.
In which words, there is a comparison instituted, and that between two parties, and two points wherein they vastly differ.

The parties are the lowly and the proud, who differ like heaven and earth: the proud are climbing up and soaring aloft; the lowly are content to creep on the ground, if that is the will of God. Let us view them more particularly as the text represents them.

On the one hand is the lowly. Here there is a line reading and a marginal, both from the Holy Spirit, and they differ only in a letter. The former is the afflicted or poor, that are low in their condition; those that have a notable crook in their lot, through affliction laid on them, whereby their condition is lowered in the world. The other is the lowly or meek humble ones, who are low in their spirit, as well as their condition, and so have their minds brought down to their lot. Both together make the character of this lowly party.

On the other hand is the proud; the gay and high minded ones. It is supposed here that they are crossed too, and have crooks in their lot; for, dividing the spoil is the consequent of a victory, and a victory presupposes a battle.

The points wherein these parties are supposed to differ, viz, being of a humble spirit, and dividing the spoil.

Afflicted and lowly ones may sometimes get their condition changed, may be raised up on high, and divide the spoil, as Hannah, Job, etc. The proud may sometimes be thrown down and crushed, as Pharaoh, Nebuchadnezzar, etc. But that is not the question. Whether it is better to be raised up with the lowly, or thrown down with the proud? There would be no difficulty in determining that. But the question is, whether it is better to be of a low and humble spirit, in low circumstances, with afflicted humble ones; or to divide the spoil, and get one's will, with the proud? If men would speak the native sentiments of their hearts, that question would be determined in a contradiction to the text. The points then here compared and set one against another, are these:

On the one hand, to be of a humble spirit with afflicted lowly ones (*Hebrew*). To be low of spirit; for the word primarily denotes lowness in situation or state: so the point here proposed is to be with, or in the state of, afflicted lowly ones, having the spirit brought down to that low lot; the lowness of the spirit balancing the lowness of one's condition.

On the other hand to divide the spoil with the proud. The point here proposed is, to be with or in the state of the proud, having their lot by main force brought to their mind; as those who, taking themselves to be injured, fight it out with the enemy, overcome and divide the spoil according to their will.

The decision made, wherein the former is preferred to the latter; 'Better it is to be of an humble spirit with the lowly than to divide the spoil with the proud'. If these two parties were set before us, it were better to take our lot with those of a low condition, who have their spirits brought as low as their lot, than with those, who, being of a proud and high spirit, have their lot brought up to their mind. A humble spirit is better than a heightened condition.

Doctrine: There is a generation of lowly afflicted ones having their spirit lowered and brought down to their lot; whose case, in that respect, is better than that of the proud getting their will, and carrying all to their mind.

The Condition of the Lowly.

We shall consider the generation of the lowly afflicted ones, having their spirit brought down to their lot. And we shall,

First, lay down some general considerations about them.

1. There is such a generation in the world, bad as the world is. The text expressly mentions them, and the scripture elsewhere speaks of them; as Psalm 9:12 and

10:12; Matthew 5:3 with Luke 6:20. Where shall we seek them? Not in heaven, there are no afflicted ones there; nor in hell, there are no lowly or humble ones there, whose spirit is brought to their lot. In this world they must then be, where the state of trial is.

2. If it were not so, Christ, as he was in the world, would have no followers in it. He was the head of that generation whom they all copy after; 'Learn of me, for I am meek and lowly of heart' (Matt. 11:29). And for his honour, and the honour of his cross, they will never be wanting while the world stands, 'Whom he did foreknow he also did predestinate to be conformed to the image of his Son' (Rom. 8:29). His image lies in these two, suffering and holiness, whereof lowliness is a chief part.

3. Nevertheless, they are certainly very rare in the world. Agur observes, that there is another generation, 'Their eyes are lofty, and their eye-lids lifted up' (Prov. 30:13) quite opposite to them, and this makes the greatest company by far. The low and afflicted lot is not so very rare, but the lowly disposition of spirit is rarely yoked with it. Many a high spirit keeps up in spite of lowering circumstances.

4. They can be no more in number than the truly godly; for nothing less than the power of divine grace can bring down men's minds from their native height, and make their will pliant to the will of God (2 Cor. 10:4, 5). Men may put on a face of submission to a low and a crossed lot, because they cannot help it, and they see it is in vain to strive; but to bring the spirit truly to it, must be the effect of humbling grace.

5. Though all the godly are of that generation, yet there are some of them to whom that character more especially belongs. The way to heaven lies through tribulation to all (Acts 14:22); and all Christ's followers are reconciled to

it notwithstanding (Luke 14:26). Yet there are some of them more remarkably disciplined than others, whose spirit is hereby humbled and brought down to their lot, 'Surely I have behaved and quieted myself as a child that is weaned of his mother; my soul is even as a weaned child' (Ps. 131:2); 'For I have learned, in whatsoever state I am, therewith to be content. I know both how to be abased, and I know how to abound; every where, and in all things I am instructed, both to be full and to be hungry, both to abound and to suffer need' (Phil. 4:11, 12).

6. A lowly disposition of soul, and habitual aim and bent of the heart that way, has a very favourable construction put upon it in heaven. Should we look for a generation perfectly purged of pride and risings of heart against their adverse lot at any time, we should find none in this world: but those who are sincerely aiming and endeavouring to reach it, and keep the way of contented submission, though sometimes blown aside, and returning to it again, God accounts to be that lowly generation (2 Cor. 7:10, 11; James 5:11).

We shall enter into particulars. There are three things which together make up their character.

Affliction in their lot. That lowly generation, preferred to the proud and prosperous, is a generation of afflicted ones, whom God keeps under the discipline of the covenant. We may take it up in these two:

1. There is a yoke of affliction of one kind or other oftentimes upon them (Ps. 73:14). God is frequently visiting them as a master doth his scholars, and a physician his patients; whereas others are in a sort overlooked by him (Rev. 3:19). They are accustomed to the yoke, and that from the time they enter into God's family (Ps. 129:1-3). God sees it good for them (Lam. 3:27, 28).

2. There is a particular yoke of affliction which God has chosen for them, that hangs about them, and is seldom, if ever, taken off them (Luke 9:23). That is their special trial, the crook in their lot, the yoke which lies on them for their constant exercise. Their other trials may be exchanged, but that is a weight that still hangs about them, bowing them down.

Lowliness in their disposition and tenor of spirit. They are a generation of lowly humble ones, whose spirits God has, by his grace, brought down from their natural height. And thus,

1. They think soberly and meanly of themselves; what they are (2 Cor. 12:9, 10); what they can do (2 Cor. 3:5); what they are worth (Gen. 32:10); and what they deserve (Lam. 3:22). Viewing themselves in the glass of the divine law and perfection, they see themselves as a mass of imperfection and sinfulness (Job 42:5, 6).

2. They think highly and honourably of God (Ps. 145:3). They are taught by the Spirit what God is; and so entertain elevated thoughts of him. They consider him as the Sovereign of the world; his perfections as infinite; his work as perfect. They look on him as the fountain of happiness, as a God in Christ, doing all things well; trusting his wisdom, goodness, and love, even where they cannot see [it] (Heb. 11:8).

3. They think favourably of others, as far as in justice they may (Phil. 2:3). Though they cannot hinder themselves from seeing their glaring faults, yet they are ready withal to acknowledge their excellencies, and esteem them so far. And, because they see more into their own mercies and advantages for holiness, and misimproving thereof, than they can see in others, they are apt to look on others as better than themselves, circumstances compared.

4. They are sunk down into a state of subordination to God and his will (Ps. 131:1, 2). Pride sets a man up against God, lowliness brings him back to his place, and lays him down at the feet of his sovereign Lord, saying, Thy will be done on earth, etc. They seek no more the command, but are content that God himself sit at the helm of their affairs, and manage all for them (Ps. 47:4).

5. They are not bent on high things, but disposed to stoop to low things (Ps. 131:1). Lowliness levels the towering imaginations, which pride mounts up against heaven; draws a veil over all personal worth and excellencies before the Lord; and yields a man's all to the Lord, to be as stepping-stones to the throne of his glory (2 Sam. 15:25, 26).

6. They are apt to magnify mercies bestowed on them (Gen. 32:10). Pride of heart overlooks and vilifies mercies one is possessed of, and fixes the eye on what is wanting in one's condition, making one like the flies, which pass over the sound places, and swarm together on the sore. On the contrary, lowliness teaches men to recount the mercies they enjoy in the lowest condition, and to set a mark on the good things they have possessed, or yet do (Job 2:10).

A Christian Response to the Crook in the Lot.
A spirit brought down to their lot. Their lot is a low and afflicted one; but their spirit is as low, being, through grace, brought down to it. We may take it up in these five things:

1. They submit to it as just, 'I will bear the indignation of the Lord, because I have sinned against him' (Micah 7:9). There are no hardships in our condition, but we have procured them to ourselves; and it is therefore just that we kiss the rod, and be silent under it, and so lower our spirits to our lot. If they complain, it is of themselves; their hearts

rise not up against the Lord, far less do they open their mouth against the heavens. They justify God, and condemn themselves, reverencing his holiness and spotless righteousness in his proceedings against them.

2. They go quietly under it as tolerable, 'It is good that a man should both hope and quietly wait for the salvation of the Lord. It is good for a man that he bear the yoke in his youth. He sitteth alone, and keepeth silence, because he hath borne it upon him; he putteth his mouth in the dust, if so be there may be hope' (Lam. 3:26-29). While the unsubdued spirit rages under the yoke as a bullock unaccustomed to it, the spirit brought to the lot, goes softly under it. They see it is of the Lord's mercies that it is not worse; they take up the naked cross, as God lays it down, without those overweights upon it that turbulent passions add thereunto; and so it becomes really more easy than they thought it could have been, like a burden fitted on the back.

3. They are satisfied in it, as drawing their comfort from another quarter than their outward condition, even as the house stands fast, when the prop is taken away that it did not lean upon. 'Although the fig-tree should not blossom, neither fruit be in the vine, yet I will rejoice in the Lord' (Hab. 3:17, 18). Thus did David in the day of his distress, 'He encouraged himself in the Lord his God' (1 Sam. 30:6). It is an argument of a spirit not brought down to the lot, when men are damped and sunk under the hardships of it, as if their condition in the world were the point whereon their happiness turned. It is want of mortification that makes men's comforts to wax and wane, ebb and flow, according to the various appearances of their lot in the world.

4. They have a complacency in it, as that which is fit and good for them (Isa. 39:8; 2 Cor. 12:10). Men have a sort of

complacency in the working of physic [medicine], though it gripes them sore; they rationally think with themselves that it is good and best for them. So these lowly souls consider their afflicted lot as a spiritual medicine, necessary, fit, and good for them; yea, best for them for the time, since it is ministered by their heavenly Father; and so they reach a holy complacency in their low afflicted lot.

The lowly spirit extracts this sweet out of the bitterness in his lot, considering how the Lord, by means of that afflicting lot, stops the provision for unruly lusts, that they may be starved; how he cuts off the by-channels, that the whole stream of the soul's love may run towards himself; how he pulls off, and holds off the man's burden and clog of earthly comforts, that he may run the more expeditiously in the way to heaven.

5. They rest in it, as what they desire not to come out of, till the God that brought them into it, sees it meet to bring them out with his good will (Isa. 28:16). Though an unsubdued spirit's time for deliverance is always ready, a humble soul will be afraid of being taken out of its afflicted lot too soon. It will not be for moving for a change, till the heaven's moving bring it about; so this hinders not prayer and the use of appointed means, with dependence on the Lord; but requires faith, hope, patience, and resignation (2 Sam. 15:25, 26).

The Proud Sinner.

We shall consider the generation of the proud getting their will, and carrying all to their mind. And in their character also are three things.

There are crosses in their lot. They also have their trials allotted them by overruling Providence, and let them be in what circumstances they will in the world, they cannot miss them altogether. For consider:

1. The confusion and vanity brought into the creation by man's sin, have made it impossible to get through the world, but men must meet with what will ruffle them (Eccles. 1:14). Sin has turned the world from a paradise into a thicket, there is no getting through without being scratched. As midges in the summer will fly about those walking abroad in a goodly attire, as well as about those in sordid apparel, so will crosses in the world meet with the high as well as the low.

2. The pride of their heart exposes them particularly to crosses. A proud heart will make a cross to itself, where a lowly soul would find none (Esther 5:13). It will make a real cross ten times the weight it would be to the humble. The generation of the proud are like nettles and thorn hedges, upon which things flying about do fix, while they pass over low and plain things; so none are more exposed to crosses than they, though none so unfit to bear them.

As appears from, [the] reigning pride in their spirit. Their spirits were never subdued by a work of thorough humiliation, they remain at the height in which the corruption of nature placed them: hence they can by no means bear the yoke God lays on them. The neck is swollen with the ill humours of pride and passion; hence, when the yoke once begins to touch it, they cannot have any more ease. We may view the case of the proud generation here in three things:

1. They have an over-value for themselves; and so will not stoop to the yoke; it is below them. What a swelling vanity is in that, 'Who is the Lord that I should obey his voice?' (Exod. 5:2). Hence a work of humiliation is necessary to make one take on the yoke, whether of Christ's precepts or

Providence. The first error is in the understanding, whence Solomon ordinarily calls a wicked man a fool; accordingly the first stroke in conversion is there too, by conviction to humble. Men are bigger in their own conceit, than they are indeed; therefore God, suiting things to what we are really, cannot please us.

2. They have an unmortified self-will, arising from that over-value for themselves, and they will not stoop (Exod. 5:2). The question between heaven and us is, whether God's will or our own must prevail? Our will is corrupt, God's will is holy; they cannot agree in one. God says in his Providence our will must yield to his; but that it will not do, till the iron sinew in it be broken (Rom. 8:7; Isa. 48:4).

3. They have a crowd of unsubdued passions taking part with self-will; and they say, he shall not stoop (Rom. 7:8, 9); and so the war begins, and there is a field of battle within and without the man (James 4:1).

A holy God crosses the self-will of proud creatures by his Providence, overruling and disposing of things contrary to their inclination; sometimes by his own immediate hand, as in the case of Cain (Gen. 4:4, 5); sometimes by the hand of men carrying things against their mind, as in the case of Ahab, to whom Naboth refused his vineyard (1 Kings 21:4).

The proud heart and will, unable to submit to the cross, or to bear to be controlled, rises up against it, and fights for the mastery, with its whole force of unmortified passions. The design is to remove the cross, even the crook, and bring the thing to their own mind: this is the cause of this unholy war, in which:

There is one black band of hellish passions that marches upward, and makes an attack on heaven itself, namely, discontent, impatience, murmuring, fretting, and the like.

'The foolishness of man perverteth his way; and his heart fretteth against the Lord' (Prov. 19:3). These fire the breast, fall the countenance (Gen. 4:6), let off sometimes a volley of indecent and passionate complaints (Jude 16) and sometimes of blasphemies (2 Kings 6:33).

There is another that marches forward, and makes an attack on the instrument or instruments of the cross, namely, anger, wrath, fury, revenge, bitterness, etc (Prov. 27:4). These carry the man out of the possession of himself (Luke 21:19), fill the heart with a boiling heat (Ps. 39:3), the mouth with clamour and evil-speaking (Eph. 4:31), and threatenings are breathed out (Acts 9:1), and sometimes set the hands on work, a most heavy event, as in the case of Ahab against Naboth.

Thus the proud carry on the war, but oftentimes they lose the day, and the cross remains immovable for all they can do; yea, and sometimes they themselves fall in the quarrel, it ends in their ruin (Exod. 15:9, 10). But that is not the case in the text.

The Spiritual Consequences of Pride.

For we are to consider them as, getting their will, and carrying all to their mind. This speaks:

1. Holy providence yielding to the man's unmortified self-will, and letting it go according to his mind (Gen. 6:3). God sees it meet to let the struggle with him fall, for it prevails not to his good (Isa. 1:5). So the reins are laid on the proud man's neck, and he has what he would be at: 'Ephraim is joined to idols, let him alone' (Hosea 4:17).

2. The lust remaining in its strength and vigour (Ps. 78:30), 'They were not estranged from their lust'. God, in the method of his covenant, sometimes gives his people

their will, and sets them where they would be; but then, in that case, the lust for the thing is mortified, and they are as weaned children (Ps. 10:17). But here the lust remains rampant: the proud seek meat for it, and get it.

3. The cross is removed, the yoke taken off (Ps. 78:29). They could not think of bringing their mind to their lot; but they thwarted with it, wrestled and fought against it, till it is brought up to their mind: so the day is their own, the victory is on their side.

4. The man is pleased in his having carried his point, even as one is when he is dividing the spoil (1 Kings 21:18, 19).

Thus the case of the afflicted lowly generation, and the proud generation prospering, is stated.

The Fruits of Humility.

Now, I am to confirm the doctrine, or the decision of the text, that the case of the former is better than that of the latter. It is better to be in a low afflicted condition, with the spirit humbled and brought down to the lot, than to be of a proud and high spirit, getting the lot brought up to it, and matters go according to one's mind. This will appear from the following considerations:

1. Humility is so far preferable to pride, that in no circumstances whatsoever its preferableness can fail. Let all the afflictions in the world attend the humble spirit, and all the prosperity in the world attend pride, humility will still have the better: as gold in a dunghill is more excellent than so much lead in a cabinet, for:

Humility is a part of the image of God. Pride is the masterpiece of the image of the devil. Let us view Him who was the express image of the Father's person, and we shall behold him meek and lowly in heart (Matt. 11:29). None more afflicted, yet his spirit perfectly brought down to his lot (Isa. 53:7), 'He was oppressed, and he was afflicted, yet he opened not his mouth'. That is a shining part of the divine image: for though God cannot be low in respect of his state and condition, yet he is of infinite condescension (Isa. 57:15). None bears as he (Rom. 2:4), nor suffers patiently so much contradiction to his will; which is proposed to us for our encouragement in affliction, as it shone in Christ. 'For consider him that endured such contradiction of sinners against himself, lest ye be wearied and faint in your minds' (Heb. 12:3).

Pride, on the other hand, is the very image of the devil (1 Tim. 3:6). Shall we value ourselves on the height of our spirits? Satan will vie with the highest of us in that point; for though he is the most miserable, yet he is the proudest in the whole creation. There is the greatest distance between his spirit and his lot; the former is as high as the throne of God, the latter as low as hell: and as it is impossible that ever his lot should be brought up to his spirit; so his spirit will never come down to his lot: and therefore he will be eternally in a state of war with his lot. Hence, even at this time, he has no rest, but goes about, seeks rest indeed, but finds none.

Now, is it not better to be like God than like the devil; like him who is the fountain of all good, than him who is the spring and sink of all evil? Can any thing possibly cast the balance here, and turn the preference to the other side? 'Then better it is to be of an humble spirit with the lowly', etc.

Humility and lowliness of spirit qualify us for friendly communion and intercourse with God in Christ. Pride makes God our enemy (1 Pet. 5:5). Our happiness here and hereafter depends on our friendly intercourse with heaven. If we have not that, nothing can make up our loss (Ps. 30:5). If we have that, nothing can make us miserable (Rom. 8:31), 'If God be for us, who can be against us?' Now, who are they whom God is for, but the humble and lowly? They who being in Christ are so made like him. He blesses them, and declares them the heirs of the crown of glory: 'Blessed are the poor in spirit, for theirs is the kingdom of heaven' (Matt. 5:3). He will look to them, be their condition ever so low, while he overlooks others (Isa. 66:2). He will have respect to them, however they be despised: 'Though the Lord be high, yet hath he respect to the lowly; but the proud he knoweth afar off' (Ps. 138:6). He will dwell with them, however poorly they dwell (Isa. 57:15). He will certainly exalt them in due time, however low they lie now (Isa. 40:4).

Whom is he against? Whom does he resist? The proud. Them he curseth (Jer. 17:5) and that curse will dry up their arm at length. The proud man is God's rival; he makes himself his own god, and would have those about him make him theirs too; he rages, he blusters, if they will not fall down before him. But God will bring him down (Isa. 40:4; Ps. 18:27).

Now, is it not better to be qualified for communion with God, than to have him engaged against us, at any rate?

Humility is a duty pleasing to God, pride a sin pleasing to the devil (Isa. 57:15; 1 Tim. 3:6). God requires us to be humble, especially under affliction, 'and be clothed with humility' (1 Pet. 5:5, 6). That is our becoming garment. The humble Publican was accepted, the proud Pharisee rejected. We may say of the generation of the proud, as 'Wrath is come upon them to the uttermost' (1 Thess. 2:16).

They please neither God nor men, but only themselves and Satan, whom they resemble in it. Now duty is better than sin at any rate.

They whose spirits are brought down to their afflicted lot, have much quiet and repose of mind, while the proud, that must have their lot brought up to their mind, have much disquiet, trouble, and vexation.

Consider here, that, on the one hand, quiet of mind, and ease within, is a great blessing, upon which the comfort of life depends. Nothing without this can make one's life happy (Dan. 5:6). And where this is maintained, nothing can make it miserable (John 16:33). This being secured in God, there is a defiance bid to all the troubles of the world (Ps. 46:2, 3) like the child sailing in the midst of the rolling waves.

The spirit brought down to the lot makes and maintains this inward tranquillity. Our whole trouble in our lot in the world rises from the disagreement of our mind therewith; let the mind be brought to the lot, and the whole tumult is instantly hushed; let it be kept in that disposition, and the man shall stand at ease in his affliction, like a rock unmoved with waters beating on it (Col. 3:15), 'And let the peace of God rule in your hearts, to the which also ye are called'.

On the other hand, consider, what disquiet of mind the proud suffer ere they can get their lot brought up to their mind. 'They have taught their tongues to speak lies, and they weary themselves to commit iniquity' (Jer. 9:5; James 4:2). 'Ye lust and have not: ye kill, and desire to have, and cannot obtain; ye fight and war, yet ye have not.' What arrows of grief go through their heart! What torture of anxiety, fretting and vexation, must they endure! What contrary passions fight within them! And what sallies [escapades] of passion do they make! What uneasiness was Haman in, before he could carry the point of revenge against Mordecai, obtaining the king's decree!

When the thing is got to their mind, it will not quit the cost. The enjoyment thereof brings not so much satisfaction and pleasure, as the want of it gave pain. This was evident in Rachel's case, as to the having of children; and in that case, Psalm 78:30, 31. There is a dead fly in the ointment that mars the savour they expected to find in it. Fruit plucked off the tree of providence, ere it is ripe, will readily set the teeth on edge. It proves like the manna kept over night (Exod. 16:20).

They have but an unsure hold of it; it does not last with them. Either it is taken from them soon, and they are just where they were again: 'I gave thee a king in my anger, and took him away in my wrath' (Hosea 13:11), having a root of pride, it quickly withers away; or else they are taken from it, that they have no access to enjoy it. So Haman obtained the decree; but ere the day of the execution came, he was gone.

They that get their spirit brought down to their afflicted lot, gain a point far more valuable than they who in their pride force up their lot to their mind, 'He that is slow in anger, is better than the mighty; and he that ruleth his spirit, than he that taketh a city' (Prov. 16:32). This will appear, if you consider:

The latter makes but a better condition in outward things, the former makes a better man. The life is more than meat - the man himself is more valuable than all external conveniences that attend him. What therefore betters the man is preferable to what betters only his condition. Who doubts but where two are sick, and the one gets himself transported from a coarse bed to a fine one, the sickness still remaining; the other lies still in the coarse bed, but the sickness is removed; that the case of the latter is preferable? So here, etc:

97

The subduing of our own passions is more excellent than to have the whole world subdued to our will: for then we are masters of ourselves, according to that (Luke 21:19). Whereas, in the other case, we are still slaves to the worst of masters (Rom. 6:16). In the one case we are safe, blow what storm will; in the other we lie exposed to thousands of dangers, 'He that hath no rule over his own spirit, is like a city that is broken down, and without walls' (Prov. 25:28).

When both shall come to be judged, it will appear the one has multiplied the tale of their good works, in bringing their spirit to their lot; the others the tale of their ill works, in bringing their lot to their spirit. We have to do with an omniscient God, in whose eyes every internal action is a work, good or bad, to be reckoned for (Rom. 2:16).

An afflicted lot is painful but, where it is well managed, it is very fruitful; it exercises the graces of the Spirit in a Christian, which otherwise would lie dormant. But there is never an act of resignation to the will of God under the cross, nor an act of trusting in him for his help, but they will be recorded in heaven's register as good works (Mal. 3:16). And these are occasioned by affliction.

On the other hand, there is never a rising of the proud heart against the lot, nor a faithless attempt to bring it to our mind, whether it succeed or not, but it passes for an ill work before God. How then will the tale of such be multiplied by the war in which the spoil is divided!

Use [application]: Of information.

1. Hence we may learn, it is not always best for folks to get their will. Many there are who cannot be pleased with God's will about them, and they get their own will with a vengeance (Ps. 81:11, 12), 'Israel would none of me, so

I gave them up to their own hearts' lusts, and they walked in their own counsels'. It may be most pleasant and grateful for the time, but it is not the safest. Let not the people pride themselves in their carrying things that way then by a strong hand; let them not triumph in such victory: the after-reckoning will open their eyes.

2. The afflicted crossed party, whose lot is kept low, is so far from being a loser, that he is a gainer thereby, if his spirit is brought down to it. And if he will see things in the light of God's unerring word, he is in better case than if he had got all carried to his mind. In the one way the vessels of wrath are fitted for destruction (Ps. 78:29-31). In the other, the vessels of mercy are fitted for glory, and so God disciplines his own (Lam. 3:27).

3. It is better to yield to Providence than to fight it out, though we should win. Yielding to the sovereign disposal is both our becoming duty and our greatest interest. Taking that way, we act most honourably; for what honour can there be in the creature's disputing his ground with his Creator? and we act most wisely; for whatever may be the success of some battles in that case, we may be sure victory will be on heaven's side in the war, 'For, by strength shall no man prevail' (1 Sam. 2:9).

4. It is of so much greater concern for us to get our spirits brought down than our outward condition raised. But who believes this? All men strive to raise their outward condition; most men never mind the bringing down of their spirits, and few there are who apply themselves to it. And what is that but to be concerned to minister drink to the thirsty sick, but never to mind to seek a cure for them, whereby their thirst may be carried off.

Use [application]: Of exhortation. As you meet with crosses in your lot in the world, let your desire be rather to have your spirit humbled and brought down, than to get the cross removed. I mean not but that you may use all lawful means for the removal of your cross, in dependence on God; but only that you be more concerned to get your spirit to bow and ply, than to get the crook in your lot evened.

Motive: It is far more needful for us to have our spirits humbled under the cross, than to have the cross removed. The removal of the cross is needful only for the ease of the flesh, the humbling for the profit of our souls, to purify them, and bring them into a state of health and cure.

The humbling of the spirit will have a mighty good effect on a crossed lot, but the removal of the cross will have none on the proud spirit. The humbling will lighten the cross mightily for the time (Matt. 11:30), and in due time carry it cleanly off (1 Pet. 5:6). But the removal of the cross is not a means to humble the proud; though it may prevent irritation, yet the disease still remains.

3. Think with yourselves how dangerous and hopeless a case it is to have the cross removed before the spirit is humbled. That is, to have the means of cure pulled away and blocked up from us, while the power of the disease is yet uncured. To be taken off trials ere we have given any good proof of ourselves, and so to be given over of our physician as hopeless (Isa. 1:5; Hosea 4:17).

Use [application]: For direction. Believing the gospel, take God for your God in Christ towards your eternal salvation, and then dwell much on the thoughts of God's greatness and holiness, and of your own sinfulness. So will you be

100

humbled under the mighty hand of God and, in due time, he will lift you up.

> Humble yourselves therefore under the mighty hand of God, that he may exalt you in due time (1 Pet. 5:6).

In the preceding part of this chapter, the apostle presents the duties of the church officers towards the people; and then the duty of the people, both towards their officers, and among themselves, which he winds up in one word, submission. For which causes he recommends humility as the great means to bring all to their respective duties. This is enforced with an argument taken from the different treatment the Lord gives to the proud and the humble; his opposing himself to the one, and showing favour to the other.

4

The Duty of Man in Affliction

Our text is an exhortation drawn from that consideration: and in it we have the duty we are to study: 'Humble yourselves therefore under the mighty hand of God, that he may exalt you in due time'. And therein we may notice:

The state of those, to whom it is proposed, those under the mighty hand of God, whom his hand has humbled, or brought low in respect of their circumstances in the world. And by these, I think, are meant, not only such as are under particular signal afflictions, which is the lot of some, but also those who, by the Providence of God, are, in any kind of way lowered, which is the lot of all. All being in a state of submission or dependence on others, God has made this life a state of trial. And for that cause he has, by his mighty hand, subjected men one to another, as wives, children, servants, to husbands, parents, masters; and these again to their superiors; among whom, again, even the highest depend on those under them, as magistrates and ministers on the people, even the supreme magistrate. This state of the world God has made for the trial of men in their several stations, and dependence on others; and therefore, when the time of trial is over, it also comes to an end. 'Then cometh the end - when he shall have put down all rule and all authority, and power' (1 Cor. 15:24, 25). Meantime, while it lasts, it makes humility necessary to all, to prompt them to the duty they owe their superiors, to whom God's mighty hand has subjected them.

The duty itself, namely, humiliation of our spirits under the humbling circumstances the Lord has placed us in. 'Humble yourselves therefore under the mighty hand of God, that he may exalt you in due time.' Whether we are under particular afflictions, which have cast us down from the height we were sometime in, or whether we are only inferiors in one or more relations; or whether, which is most common, both these are in our case, we must therein eye the mighty hand of God, as that which placed us there, and is over us, there to hold us down in it. And so, with an awful regard thereto, bow down under it in the temper and disposition of our spirits, suiting our spirits to our lot, and careful of performing the duty of our low sphere.

A particular spring of this duty; therefore we must consider, that those who cannot quietly keep the place assigned them of God in their afflictions or relations, but still press upward against the mighty hand that is over them. That mighty hand, resists them, throwing them down, and often farther down than before; whereas, it treats them with grace and favour, that compose themselves under it, to a quiet discharge of their duty in their situation; so, eyeing [considering] this, we must set ourselves to humble ourselves.

The infallible issue of that course; that he may exalt you in due time. The particle *that*, is not always to be understood finally, as denoting the end or design the agent proposes to himself,

104

but sometimes eventually only, as denoting the event or issue of the action (John 9:2, 3; 1 John 2:19). So here, the meaning is not, humble yourselves, on design he may exalt you; but, and it shall issue in his exalting you. Compare James 4:10.

Here is a happy event, of humiliation of spirit secured, and that is exaltation or lifting up on high, by the power of God, that he may exalt you. Exalting will as surely follow on humiliation of spirit, suitable to the low lot, as the morning follows the night, or the sun rises after the dawn. And these words are fitted to obviate the objections that the world and our corrupt hearts are apt to make against bringing down the spirit to the low lot.

Objection: If we let our spirit fall, we shall lie always at folks' feet, and they will trample on us.

Answer: No; pride of spirit unsubdued, will bring men to lie at the feet of others forever (Isa. 66:24). But humiliation of spirit will bring them undoubtedly out from under their feet (Mal. 4:2, 3). They that humble themselves now will be exalted forever; they will be brought out of their low situation and circumstances. Cast yourselves even down with your low lot, and assure yourselves you shall not lie there.

Objection: If we do not raise ourselves, none will raise us; and therefore we must see to ourselves, to do ourselves right.

Answer: That is wrong. Humble ye yourselves in respect of your spirits, and God will raise you up in respect of your lot, or low condition; and they that have God engaged for raising them, have no reason to say they have none to do it for them. Bringing down of the spirit is our duty, raising us up is God's work; let us not forfeit the privilege of God's raising us up, by arrogating that work to ourselves, taking it out of his hand.

Objection: But sure we shall never rise high, if we let our spirits fall.

Answer: That is wrong too: God will not only raise the humble ones, but he will lift them up on high; for so the word signifies. They shall be as high at length as ever they were low, were they ever so low; no, the exaltation will [be in] proportion to the humiliation.

Here is the date of that happy event when it will fall out. In due time, or in the season, the proper season for it (Gal. 6:9), 'In due season we shall reap, if we faint not'. We are apt to weary in humbling trying circumstances, and would instantly have up our head (John 7:6). But Solomon observes, there is a time for every thing when it does best, and the wise will wait for it (Eccles. 3:1-8). There is a time too for exalting them that humble themselves; God has set it, and it is the due time for the purpose, the time when it does best, even as sowing in the spring, and reaping in the harvest. When that time comes, your exalting shall no longer be put off, and it would come too soon should it come before that time.

Submitting to the Will of God.

Doctrine: The bent of one's heart, in humbling circumstances, should lie towards a suitable humbling of the spirit, as under God's mighty hand placing us in them. We shall consider, what things are supposed in this.

1. It supposes that God brings men into humbling circumstances, 'And all the trees of the field shall know, that I the Lord have brought down the high tree' (Ezek. 17:24). There is a root of pride in the hearts of all men on earth, that must be mortified ere they can be meet for heaven; and therefore no man can miss, in this time of trial, some things that will give a proof whether he can stoop or no. And God brings them into humbling circumstances for that very end, 'The Lord thy God led thee these forty years in

the wilderness, to humble thee, and to prove thee, to know what was in thine heart' (Deut. 8:2).

2. These circumstances prove pressing as a weight on the heart, tending to bear it down, 'Therefore he brought down their hearts with labour' (Ps. 107:12). They strike at the grain of the heart, and cross the natural inclination: whence a trial arises, whether, when God lays on his mighty hand, the man can yield under it or not; and consequently, whether he is meet for heaven or not.

3. The heart is naturally apt to rise up against these humbling circumstances, and consequently against the mighty hand that brings and keeps them on. The man naturally bends his force to get off the weight, that he may get up his head, seeking more to please himself than to please his God, 'They cry out by reason of the arm of the mighty: but none saith, Where is God my Maker?' (Job 35:9, 10). This is the first gate the heart runs to in humbling circumstances; and in this way the unsubdued spirit holds on.

4. But what God requires is, rather to labour to bring down the heart, than to get up the head (James 4:10). Here lies the proof of one's meetness for heaven; and then is one in the way heaven-ward, when he is more concerned to get down his heart than to get up his head, to go calmly under his burden than to get it off, to bow under the mighty hand, than to put it off him.

5. There must be a noticing of the hand of God in humbling circumstances; 'Here ye the rod, and him who hath appointed it' (Micah 6:9). There is an abjectness of spirit, whereby some give up themselves to the will of others in the harshest treatment, merely to please them, without regard to the authority and command of God. This is real meanness of spirit, whereby one lies quietly to be trampled on

by a fellow worm, from its imaginary weight; and none so readily fall into it as the proud, at some times, to serve their own turn. These are men-pleasers (Eph. 6:6, with Gal. 1:10).

What are those humbling circumstances the mighty hand of God brings men into? Supposing here what was before taught concerning the crook in the lot being of God's making, these are circumstances:

1. *Of imperfection*: God has placed all men in such circumstances under a variety of wants and imperfections (Phil. 3:12). We can look no where, where we are not beset with them. There is a heap of natural and moral imperfections about us: our bodies and our souls, in all their faculties, are in a state of imperfection. The pride of all glory is stained; and it is a shame for us not to be humbled under such wants as attend us; it is like a beggar strutting in his rags.

2. *Of inferiority in relations*, whereby men are set in the lower place in relations and society, and made to depend on others (1 Cor. 7:24). God has, for a trial of men's submission to himself, subjected them to others whom he has set over them, to discover what regard they will pay to his authority and commands at second hand. Dominion or superiority is a part of the divine image shining in them (1 Cor. 11:7). And therefore reverence of them, consisting in an awful regard to that ray of the divine image shining in them, is necessarily required (Eph. 5:23; Heb. 12:9). The same holds in all other relations and superiorities, namely, that they are so far in the place of God to their relatives (Ps. 82:6) and though the parties be worthless in themselves, that looses not from the debt due to them (Acts 23:4, 5; Rom. 13:7). The reason is, because it is not their qualities, but their character, which is the ground of that debt of reverence

and subjection; and the trial God takes of us in that matter turns not on the point of the former, but of the latter.

Now, God having placed us in these circumstances of inferiority, all refractoriness, in all things not contrary to the command of God, is a rising up against his mighty hand (Rom. 13:2), because it is immediately upon us for that effect, though it is a man's hand that is immediately on us.

3. *Of contradiction*, tending directly to balk us of our will. This was a part of our Lord's state of humiliation, and the apostle supposes it will be a part of ours too (Heb. 12:3). There is a perfect harmony in heaven, no one to contradict another there: for they are in their state of retribution and exaltation: but we are here in our state of trial and humiliation, and therefore cannot miss contradiction, be we placed ever so high.

Whether these contradictions be just or unjust, God tries men with them to humble them, to break them off from addiction to their own will, and to teach them resignation and self-denial. They are in their own nature humbling, and much the same to us, as the breaking of a horse or a bullock is to them. And I believe there are many cases in which there can be no accounting for them, but by recurring to this use God has for them.

4. *Of affliction* (Prov. 16:19). Prosperity puffs up sinners with pride; for it is very hard to keep a low spirit with a high and prosperous lot. But God, by affliction, calls men down from their heights to sit in the dust, plucks away their gay feathers wherein they prided themselves, rubs the paint and varnish from off the creature, whereby it appears more in its native deformity. There are various kinds of affliction, some more, some less humbling, but all of them are humbling.

Wherefore, not to lower the spirit under the affliction, is to attempt to rise up when God is casting and holding us down; and cannot fail, if continued in, to provoke the Lord to break us in pieces (Ezek. 24:13). For the afflicting hand of God is mighty.

5. *Of sin*: as the punishment of sin. We may allude to that (Job 30:19). All the sin in the world is a punishment of Adam's first sin. Man threw himself into the mire at first, and now he is justly left weltering in it. Men willfully make one false step, and for that cause they are justly left to make another worse; and sin hangs about all, even the best. And this is over-ruled of God for our humiliation, that we may be ashamed, and never open our mouth any more. Wherefore, not to be humbled under our sinfulness, is to rise up against the mighty hand of God, and to justify all our sinful departing from Him, as lost to all sense of duty, and void of shame.

Humbling Ourselves Under God.

What it is in humbling circumstances, to humble ourselves under the mighty hand of God. This is the great thing to be aimed at in our humbling circumstances. And we may take it up in these eight things:

1. *Noticing God's mighty hand*, as employed in bringing about every thing that concerns us, either in the way of efficacy or permission, 'And he said, "It is the Lord; let him do what seemeth him good"' (1 Sam. 3:18). 'And the king said, "The Lord hath said unto him, 'Curse David': who shall then say, 'wherefore hast thou done so?'"' (2 Sam. 16:10). He is the fountain of all perfection, but we must trace our imperfections to his sovereign will. It is he that has posted every one in their relations by his Providence; without him we could not meet with such contradictions; for, 'The king's heart is in the hand of the Lord, as the rivers of water: he turneth it whithersoever he pleaseth' (Prov. 21:1). He sends afflictions, and justly punishes one sin with another (Isa. 6:10).

2. *A sense of our own worthlessness and nothingness before him* (Ps. 144:3). Looking to the infinite Majesty of the mighty hand dealing with us, we should say, with Abraham, 'Behold, I am but dust and ashes' (Gen. 18:27); and say amen to the cry (Isa. 40:6). All flesh is grass, etc. The keeping up of thoughts of our own excellence, under the pressure of God's mighty hand, is the very thing that swells the heart in pride, causing it to rise up against it. And it is the letting of all such thoughts of ourselves fall before the eyes of his glory, that is the humbling required.

3. *A sense of our guilt and filthiness* (Rom. 3:10; Isa. 64:6). The mighty hand does not press us down, but as sinners, it is meet then that under it we see our sinfulness. Our guilt, whereby we shall appear criminals justly caused to suffer; our filthiness, whereupon we may be brought to loathe ourselves; and then we shall think nothing lays us lower than we well deserve. It is the overlooking our sinfulness that suffers the proud heart to swell.

4. *A silent submission under the hand of God.* His sovereignty challenges this of us, 'Nay, but, O man, who art thou that repliest against God?' (Rom. 9:20). And nothing but unsubdued pride of spirit can allow us to answer again under his sovereign hand. A view of his sovereignty humbled and awed the Psalmist into submission, with a profound silence, 'I was dumb, I opened not my mouth, because thou didst it' (Ps. 39:9). 'The Lord gave, and the Lord hath taken away; blessed be the name of the Lord' (Job 1:21). And 40:4, 5: 'What shall I answer thee? I will lay mine hand upon my mouth. Once have I spoken, but I will proceed no farther.' And Eli, 'It is the Lord; let him do what seemeth him good' (1 Sam. 3:18).

5. *A magnifying of his mercies towards us in the midst of all his proceedings against us* (Ps. 144:3). Has he laid us low? If we be duly humbled, we shall wonder he has laid us no lower

(Ezra 9:13). For however low the humble are laid, they will see they are not yet so low as their sins deserve (Lam. 3:22).

6. *A holy and silent admiration of the ways and counsels of God, as to us unsearchable* (Rom. 11:33). Pride of heart thinks nothing too high for the man, and so arraigns before its tribunal the divine proceedings, pretends to see through them, censures freely and condemns. But humiliation of spirit disposes a man to think awfully and honourably of those mysteries of Providence he is not able to see through.

7. *A forgetting and laying aside before the Lord all our dignity, whereby we excel others* (Rev. 4:10). Pride feeds itself on the man's real or imaginary personal excellence and dignity, and, being so inured to it before others, cannot forget it before God (Luke 18:11), 'God, I thank thee I am not as other men'. But humiliation of spirit makes it all to vanish before him as does the shadow before the shining sun, and it lays the man, in his own eyes, lower than any. 'Surely I am more brutish than any man, and have not the understanding of a man' (Prov. 30:2).

8. *A submitting readily to the meanest offices requisite or agreeable to our circumstances.* Pride at every turn finds something that is below the man to condescend or stoop to, measuring by his own mind and will, not by the circumstances in which God has placed him. But humility measures by the circumstances one is placed in, and readily falls in with what they require. Hereof our Saviour gave us an example to be imitated (Phil. 2:8), 'Being found in fashion as a man he humbled himself, and became obedient unto death'. 'If I then, your Lord and Master, have washed your feet, ye ought also to wash one another's feet' (John 13:14).

Use [application]: Of exhortation: let the bent of your heart then, in all your humbling circumstances, be towards the humbling of your spirit, as under the mighty hand of God. This lies in two things:

1. Carefully notice all your humbling circumstances, and overlook none of them. Observe your imperfections; inferiority in relations; contradictions you meet with; your afflictions; uncertainty of all things about you; and your sinfulness. Look through them carefully, and consider the steps of the conduct of Providence toward you in these, that you may know yourselves, and may not be strangers at home, blind to your own real state and case.

2. Observe what these circumstances require of you, as suitable to them; bend your endeavour towards it, to bring your spirits into that temper of humiliation, that, as your lot is really low in all these respects, so your spirits may be low too, as under the mighty hand of God. Let this be your great aim through your whole life, and your exercise every day.

Motive:

1. God is certainly at work to humble one and all of us. However high any are lifted up in this world, Providence has hung certain badges for humiliation on them, whether they will notice them or not (Isa. 40:6). Now, it is our duty to fall in with the design of Providence, that while God is humbling us, we may be humbling ourselves, and that we may not receive humbling dispensations in vain.

2. The humiliation of our spirit will not take effect without our own agency therein: while God is working on us that way, we must work together with him; for he works on us as rational agents, who being moved, move themselves (Phil. 2:12, 13). God by his Providence may force down our lot and condition without us, but the spirit must come down voluntarily and of choice, or not at all. Therefore,

113

strike in with humbling Providence in humbling yourselves, as mariners spread out the sails when the wind begins to blow, that they may go away before it.

3. If you do not, you resist the mighty hand of God (Acts 7:51). Ye resist in so far as you do not yield, but stand as a rock keeping your ground against your Maker in humbling providence, 'Thou hast stricken them, but they have not grieved; thou hast consumed them, but they have refused to receive correction. They have made their faces harder than a rock; they have refused to return' (Jer. 5:3). Much more when you work against him to force up your condition, which you may see God means to hold down.

And of this resistance consider, the sinfulness; what an evil thing it is. It is a direct fighting against God, a shaking off of subjection to our sovereign Lord, and a rising in rebellion against him (Isa. 45:9).

The folly of it: how unequal is the match! How can the struggle end well? (Job 9:4). What else can possibly be the issue of the potsherds of the earth dashing against the Rock of ages, but that they are broken to pieces? All men must certainly bow or break under the mighty hand of God (Job 41:8).

A Season for Humbling Ourselves.

4. This is the time of humiliation, even the time of this life. Every thing is beautiful in its season; and the bringing down of the spirit now is beautiful, as in the time thereof, even as the plowing and sowing of the ground is in the spring. Consider:

Humiliation of spirit is in the sight of God of great price (1 Pet. 3:4). As he has a special aversion to pride of heart, he has a special liking of humility (ch. 5:5). The humbling of sinners and bringing them down from their heights, wherein the corruption of their nature has set them, is the great end of his word, and of His Providence.

It is no easy thing to humble men's spirits; it is not a little that will do it; it is a work that is not soon done. There is need of a digging deep for a thorough humiliation in the work of conversion (Luke 6:48). Many a stroke must be given at the root of the tree of the natural pride of heart before it falls. Oftentimes it seems to be fallen, and yet, it arises again. And, even when the root stroke is given in believers, the rod of pride buds again, so that there is still occasion for new humbling work.

The whole time of this life is appointed for humiliation. This was signified by the forty years the Israelites had in the wilderness (Deut. 8:2). It was so to Christ, and therefore it must be so to men (Heb. 12:2). And in that time they must either be formed according to his image, or else appear as reprobate silver that will not take it on by any means (Rom. 8:29). So that whatever lifting up men may now and then get in this life, the habitual course of it will still be humbling.

There is no humbling after this (Rev. 22:11). If the pride of the heart is not brought down in this life, it will never be; no kindly humiliation is to be expected in the other life. There the proud will be broken in pieces, but not softened; their lot and condition will be brought to the lowest pass, but the pride of their spirits will still remain, whence they will be in eternal agonies through the opposition betwixt their spirits and lot (Rev. 16:21).

Wherefore, beware lest you sit [out] your time of humiliation. Humbled we must be, or we are gone forever. And this is the time, the only time of it; therefore, make your hay while the sun shines; strike in with humbling Providence, and fight not against them while you have them (Acts 13:41). The season of grace will not last; if you sleep in seed time, you will beg in harvest.

5. This is the way to turn humbling circumstances to a good account; so that instead of being losers you would be gainers by them (Ps. 119:71), 'It is good for me that I have been afflicted'. Would you gather grapes of these thorns and thistles, set yourselves to get your spirits humbled by them.

Humiliation of spirit is a most valuable thing in itself (Prov.16:32). It cannot be bought too dear. Whatever one is made to suffer, if his spirit is thereby duly brought down, he has what is well worth bearing all the hardship for (1 Pet. 3:4).

Humility of spirit brings many advantages along with it. It is a fruitful bough, well laden, wherever it is. It contributes to one's ease under the cross (Matt. 11:30; Lam. 3:27-29). It is a sacrifice particularly acceptable to God (Ps. 51:17). The eye of God is particularly on such for good, 'To this man will I look, even to him that is poor, and of a contrite spirit, and trembleth at my word' (Isa. 66:2). Yea he dwells with them (Isa. 57:15). And it carries a line of wisdom through one's whole conduct, 'With the lowly is wisdom' (Prov. 11:2).

6. Consider it is a mighty hand that is at work with us; the hand of the mighty God; let us then bend our spirits towards a compliance with it, and not wrestle against it.

We must fall under it: since the design of it is to bring us down, we cannot stand before it; for it cannot miscarry in its designs (Isa. 46:10), 'My counsel shall stand'. So fall before it we must, either in the way of duty or judgment, 'Thine arrows are sharp in the heart of the king's enemies, whereby the people fall under thee' (Ps. 46:5).

They that are so wise as to fall in humiliation under the mighty hand, be they ever so low the same hand will raise them up again (James 4:10). In a word, be the proud ever so high, God will bring them down: be the humble ever so low, God will raise them up.

5

Directions for Reaching This Humiliation

General Directions.

1. Fix it in your heart to seek some spiritual improvement of the conduct of Providence towards you (Micah 6:9). Till once your heart gets set that way, your humiliation is not to be expected (Hosea 14:9). But nothing is more reasonable, if we would act either like men or Christians, than to aim at turning what is so grievous to the flesh unto the profit of the spirit; that if we are losers on one hand, we may be gainers on another.

2. Settle the matter of your eternal salvation, in the first place, by betaking yourself to Christ, and taking God for your God in him, according to the gospel-offer (Hosea 2:19; Heb. 8:10). Let your humbling circumstances move you to this, that while the creature dries up, you may go to the fountain: for it is impossible to reach due humiliation under his mighty hand, without faith in him as your God and friend (Heb. 11:6; 1 John 4:19).

3. Use the means of soul-humbling in the faith of the promise (Ps. 28:7). Moses, smiting the rock in faith of the promise, made water gush out, which otherwise would not at all have appeared. Let us do likewise in dealing with our rocky hearts. They must be laid on the soft bed of the gospel, and struck there, as Joel 2:13, 'Turn to the Lord your God, for he is gracious and merciful'; or they will never kindly break or fall in humiliation.

Particular Directions.

1. Assure yourselves that there are no circumstances that you are in so humbling, but you may get your heart acceptably brought down to them (1 Cor. 10:13), 'But God is faithful, who will not suffer you to be tempted above that ye are able, but will with the temptation also make a way to escape, that ye may be able to bear it'. This is truth (2 Cor. 12:9), 'My grace is sufficient for thee; for my strength is made perfect in weakness'. And you should be persuaded of it, with application to yourselves, if ever you would reach the end. 'I can do all things through Christ which strengtheneth me' (Phil. 4:13). God allows you to be persuaded of it, whatever is your weakness and the difficulty of the task. 'For our sakes this is written, that he that ploweth should plow in hope; and he that thresheth in hope, should be partaker of his hope' (1 Cor. 9:10). And the belief thereof is a piece of the life of faith (2 Tim. 2:1). If you have no hope of success, your endeavours, as they will be heartless, so they will be vain. 'Wherefore lift up the hands that hang down, and the feeble knees' (Heb. 12:12).

2. Whatever hand is, or is not, in your humbling circumstances, do you take God for your party, and consider yourselves therein as under his mighty hand (Micah 6:9). Men in their humbling circumstances overlook God; so

they find not themselves called to humility under them; they fix their eyes on the creature instrument, and instead of humility, their hearts rise. But take him for your party that ye may remember the battle, and do no more (Job 41:8).

3. Be much in the thoughts of God's infinite greatness; consider his holiness and majesty, to awe you into the deepest humiliations (Isa. 6:3-5). Job met with many humbling providences in his case, but he was never sufficiently humbled under them, till the Lord made a new discovery of himself unto him, in his infinite majesty and greatness. He kept his ground against his friends, and stood to his points, till the Lord took that method with him. It was begun with thunder (Job 37:1, 2). Then followed God's voice out of the whirlwind (chapter 38:1), whereon Job is brought down (ch. 40:4, 5). It is renewed till he is farther humbled (ch. 42:5, 6), 'Wherefore I abhor myself, and repent in dust and ashes'.

4. Inure yourselves silently to admit mysteries in the conduct of Providence towards you, which you are not able to comprehend, but will adore (Rom. 11:33), 'O the depth of the riches, both of the wisdom and knowledge of God! How unsearchable are his judgments, and his ways past finding out!' That was the first word God said to Job (38:2), 'Who is this that darkeneth counsel by words without knowledge?' It went to his heart, stuck with him, and he comes over it again (ch. 42:3), as that which particularly brought him to his knees, to the dust. Even in those steps of Providence, which we seem to see far into, we may well allow there are some mysteries beyond what we see. And in those which are perplexing and puzzling, sovereignty should silence us; his infinite wisdom should satisfy, though we cannot see.

5. Be much in the thoughts of your own sinfulness (Job 40:4), 'Behold I am vile, what shall I answer thee?

I will lay mine hand upon my mouth'. It is overlooking of that which gives us so much ado with humbling circumstances. While the eyes are held that they cannot see sin, the heart riseth against them; but when they are opened, it falls. Wherefore, whenever God is dealing with you in humbling dispensations, turn your eyes, upon that occasion, on the sinfulness of your nature, heart, and life, and that will help forward your humiliation.

6. Settle it in your heart, that there is need of all the humbling circumstances you are put in. This is truth (1 Pet. 1:6), 'Though now for a season (if need be) ye are in heaviness through manifold temptations'. God brings no needless trials upon us, afflicts none but as their need requires (Lam. 3:33), 'For he doth not afflict willingly, nor grieve the children of men'. That is an observable difference betwixt our earthly and our heavenly Father's correction (Heb. 12:10), 'They, after their own pleasure; but he for our profit, that we might be partakers of his holiness'. Look to the temper of your own hearts and nature, how apt to be lifted up, to forget God, to be carried away with the vanities of the world: what foolishness is bound up in your heart! Thus you will see the need of humbling circumstances for ballast, and of the rod for the fool's back; and if at any time you cannot see that need, believe it on the ground of God's infinite wisdom, that does nothing in vain.

7. Believe a kind design of Providence in them towards you. God calls us to this, as the key that opens the heart under them (Rev. 3:19). Satan suggests suspicions to the contrary, as the bar which may hold it shut, 'This evil is of the Lord, why should I wait for the Lord any longer?' (2 Kings 6:33) As long as the suspicion of an ill design in them against us reigns, the creature will, like the worm at

the man's feet, put itself in the best posture of defence it can, and harden itself in sorrow: but the faith of a kind design will cause it to open out itself in humility before him.

Case [illustration]: 'O! If I knew there were a kind design in it, I would willingly bear it, although there were more of it; but I fear a ruining design of Providence against me therein'.

Answer: Now, what word of God, or discovery from heaven, have you to ground these fears upon? None at all, but from hell (1 Cor. 10:13). What think you the design towards you in the gospel is? Can you believe no kind design in all the words of grace there heaped up? What is that, I pray, but black unbelief in its hue of hell, flying in the face of the truth of God, and making him a liar (Isa. 55:1; 1 John 5:10, 11). The gospel is a breathing of love and goodwill to the world of mankind sinners (Titus 2:11, 3:3-4; 1 John 4:14; John 3:17). But you believe it not, in that case, more than devils believe it. If you can believe a kind design there, you must believe it in your humbling circumstances too; for the design of Providence cannot be contrary to the design of the gospel; but contrariwise, the latter is to help forward to the other.

8. Think with yourselves, that this life is the time of trial for heaven, 'Blessed is the man that endureth temptation; for when he is tried, he shall receive the crown of life, which the Lord hath promised to them that love him' (James 1:12). And therefore there should be a welcoming of humbling circumstances in that view (v. 2), 'Count it all joy when ye fall into divers temptations'. If there is an honourable office, or beneficial employment to be bestowed, men strive to be taken on trial for it, in hope they may be thereupon legally admitted to it. Now God takes trial of men for heaven by humbling circumstances, as the whole Bible teacheth; and shall men be so very slow to stoop to them?

121

The Future Glory of the Believer.

I would ask you, is it nothing to you to stand a candidate for glory, to be put on trial for heaven? Is there not an honour in it, an honour that all the saints have had? 'Behold we count them happy that endure' (James 5:10, 11). And a fair prospect in it, 'For our light affliction, which is but for a moment, worketh for us a far more exceeding and eternal weight of glory' (2 Cor. 4:17). Do but put the case, that God should overlook you as one whom it is needless ever to try on that head; that he should order you your portion in this life with full ease, as one that is to get no more of him; what would that be?

What a vast disproportion is there between your trials and the future glory! Your most humbling circumstances, how light are they in comparison of the weight of it! The longest continuance of them is but for a moment, compared with that eternal weight. Alas! there is much unbelief at the root of all our uneasiness under our humbling circumstances. Had we a clearer view of the other world, we should not make so much of either the smiles or frowns of this.

What do you think of coming off foul in the trial of your humbling circumstances? 'The lead is consumed of the fire; the founder melteth in vain; for the wicked are not plucked away. Reprobate silver shall men call them, because the Lord hath rejected them' (Jer. 6:29, 30). That the issue of it be only, that your heart appear of such a temper as by no means to be humbled; and that therefore you must and shall be taken off them, while yet no humbling appears. I think the awfulness of the dispensation is such, as might set us to our knees to deprecate the lifting us up from our humbling circumstances, ere our hearts are humbled (Isa. 1:5; Ezek. 24:13).

9. Think with yourselves, how, by humbling circumstances, the Lord prepares us for heaven, 'Giving thanks unto the Father, who hath made us meet to be partakers of the inheritance of the saints in light' (Col. 1:12; 2 Cor. 5:5). The stones and timber are laid down, turned over and over, and hewed, ere they be set up in the building; and not set up just as they come out of the quarry and wood. Were they capable of a choice, such of them as would refuse the iron tool would be refused a place in the building. Pray, how do you think you are made meet for heaven, by the warm sunshine of this world's ease, and getting all your will here? No, Sir, that would put your mouth out of taste for the joys of the other world. Vessels of dishonour are fitted for destruction that way; but vessels of honour for glory by humbling circumstances.

I would say here, will nothing please you but two heavens, one here, another hereafter? God has secured one heaven for the saints, one place where they shall get all their will, wish, and desire; where there shall be no weight on them to hold them down; and that is in the other world. But you must have it both here and there, or you cannot digest it. Why do you not quarrel too, that there are not two summers in one year; two days in the twenty-four hours? The order of the one heaven is as firm as that of the years and days, and you can not reverse it: therefore, choose you whether you will take your night or your day first, your winter or your summer, your heaven here or hereafter.

Without being humbled with humbling circumstances in this life, ye are not capable of heaven, 'Now, he that hath wrought us for the self-same thing is God' (2 Cor. 5:5). You may indeed lie at ease here in a bed of sloth and dream of heaven, big with hopes of a fool's paradise, wishing to cast yourselves just out of Delilah's lap into Abraham's bosom.

Heaven.

But except you be humbled, you are not capable, of the Bible-heaven, that heaven described in the Old and New Testaments. Is not that heaven a lifting up in due time? But, how shall you be lifted up that are never well got down? Where will your tears be to be wiped away? What place will there be for your triumph, who will not fight the good fight? How can it be a rest to you, who cannot submit to labour?

The Saints' Heaven.

Of the saints' heaven: 'And he said unto me, These are they which came out of great tribulation, and have washed their robes, and made them white in the blood of the Lamb' (Rev. 7:14). This answers the question about Abraham, Isaac, and Jacob, and all the saints with them there: they were brought down to the dust by humbling circumstances, and out of these they came before the throne. How can you ever think to be lifted up with them, with whom you cannot think to be brought down?

Christ's Heaven.

Of Christ's heaven: 'Who for the joy that was set before him, endured the cross, despising the shame, and is now set down at the right hand of God' (Heb. 12:2). O! Consider how the Forerunner made his way, 'Ought not Christ to have suffered these things, and to enter into his glory?' (Luke 24:26). And lay your account with it, that if you get where He is, you must go thither as he went, 'And he said, "If any man will come after me, let him deny himself, and take up his cross daily, and follow me"' (Luke 9:23).

10. Give up at length with your towering hopes from this world, and confine them to the world to come. Be as pilgrims and strangers here, looking for your rest in heaven, and not till

you come there. There is a prevailing evil, 'Thou art wearied in the greatness of thy way: yet saidst thou not, "There is no hope"' (Isa. 57:10). So the Babel-building is still continued, though it has fallen down again and again: for men say, 'The bricks are fallen down, but we will build with hewn stones; the sycamores are cut down, but we will change them into cedars' (Isa. 9:10). This makes humbling work very long; we are so hard to quit hold of the creature, to fall off from the breast and be weaned: but fasten on the other world, and let your hold of this go; so shall you 'be humbled' indeed under 'the mighty hand'. The faster you hold the happiness of that world, the easier will it be to accommodate yourselves to your humbling circumstances here.

11. Make use of Christ in all his offices, for your humiliation under your humbling circumstances. That only is kindly humiliation that comes in this way, 'And they shall look upon me whom they have pierced, and they shall mourn' (Zech. 12:10). This you must do by trusting on him for that effect:

1. As a *Priest* for you. You have a conscience full of guilt, and that will make one uneasy in any circumstances; and far more in humbling circumstances; it will be like a thorn in the shoulder on which a burden is laid. But the blood of Christ will purge the conscience, draw out the thorn, give ease (Isa. 33:24), and fit for service, doing or suffering (Heb. 9:14), 'How much more shall the blood of Christ ... purge your conscience from dead works to serve the living God?'

2. As your *Prophet* to teach you. We have need to be taught rightly to discern our humbling circumstances; for, often we mistake them so far, that they prove an oppressive load; whereas, could we rightly see them, just as God sets them to us, they would be humbling, but not so oppressive. Truly

125

we need Christ, and the light of his word and Spirit, to let us see our cross and trial as well as our duty (Ps. 25:9, 10).

3. And as your *King*. You have a stiff heart, loth to bow, even in humbling circumstances: take a lesson from Moses what to do in such a case, 'And he said, "Let my Lord, I pray thee, go amongst us (for it is a stiff-necked people), and pardon our iniquity and our sin"' (Exod. 34:9). Put it in his hand that is strong and mighty (Ps. 24:8). He is able to cause it to melt, and, like wax before the fire, turn to the seal.

Think on these directions, in order to put them in practice, remembering: if you know these things, happy are you if you do them. Remember humbling work is a work that will fill your hand, while you live here, and that you cannot come to the end of it till death; and humbling circumstances will attend you, while you are in this lower world. A change of them you may get; but a freedom from them you cannot, till you come to heaven. So the humbling circumstances of our imperfections, relations, contradictions, afflictions, uncertainties, and sinfulness, will afford matter of exercise to us while here. What remains of the purpose of this text, I shall comprise in:

A Promise of Blessing for the Afflicted.

Doctrine: There is a due time, wherein those that now humble themselves under the mighty hand of God will certainly be lifted up.

1. Those who shall share of this lifting up, must pay their account, in the first place, with a casting down (Rev. 7:14; John 16:33), 'In the world ye shall have tribulation'. There is no coming to the Promised Land, according to the settled method of grace, but through the wilderness; nor entering into this exaltation, but through a strait gate. If we cannot away with the casting down, we shall not taste the sweet of the lifting up.

2. Being cast down by the mighty hand of God, we must learn to lie still and quiet under it, till the same hand that cast us down raise us up, if we would share of this promised lifting up (Lam. 3:27). It is not the being cast down into humbling circumstances, by the Providence of God, but the coming down of our spirits under them, by the grace of God, that brings us within the compass of this promise.

3. Those who are never humbled in humbling circumstances shall never be lifted up in the way of this promise. Men may keep their spirits on the high bend in their humbling circumstances, and in that case may get a lifting up (Prov. 16:19); but such a lifting up, as will end in a more grievous fall. 'Surely thou didst set them in slippery places, thou castedst them down in a moment' (Ps. 73:18). But they who will not humble themselves in humbling circumstances, will find that their obstinacy will keep their misery ever fast on them without remedy.

4. Humility of spirit, in humbling circumstances, ascertains a lifting up out of them some time, with the good-will and favour of heaven, 'I tell you this man went down to his house justified rather than the other; for every one that exalteth himself shall be abased, and he that humbleth himself shall be exalted' (Luke 18:14). Solomon observes, that 'a soft answer turneth away wrath; but grievous words stir up anger' (Prov. 15:1). And so it is, that while the proud, through their obstinacy, do but wreathe the yoke faster about their own necks, the humble ones, by their yielding, make their relief sure, 'He raiseth up the poor out of the dust, and lifteth up the beggar from the dunghill, to set them among princes, and to make them inherit the throne of glory. He will keep the feet of his saints, and the wicked shall be silent in darkness; for by strength shall no

man prevail. The adversaries of the Lord shall be broken in pieces' (1 Sam. 2:8-10). So cannon will break down a stone wall, while yielding packs of wool will take away its force.

5. There is an appointed time for the lifting up of those that humble themselves in their humbling circumstances, 'For the vision is yet for an appointed time, but at the end it shall speak and not lie: though it tarry, wait for it; because it will surely come, it will not tarry' (Hab. 2:3). To every thing there is a time, as for humbling, so for lifting up (Eccles. 3:3). We know it not, but God knows it, who has appointed it. Let not the humble one say, I shall never be lifted up. There is a time fixed for it, as precisely as for the rising of the sun after a long and dark night, or the return of the spring after a long and sharp winter.

6. It is not to be expected, that immediately upon one's humbling himself, the lifting up is to follow. No: one is not merely to lie down under the mighty hand, but to lie still, waiting the due time; humbling work is long work; the Israelites had forty years of it in the wilderness. God's people must be brought to put a blank in his hand, as to the time; and while they have a long night of walking in darkness, must trust, 'Who is among you, that feareth the Lord, that obeyeth the voice of his servant, that walketh in darkness and hath no light? Let him trust in the name of the Lord, and stay upon his God' (Isa. 50:10).

7. The appointed time for the lifting up is the due time, the time fittest for it, wherein it will come most seasonably. 'And let us not be weary in well-doing; for, in due season we shall reap, if we faint not' (Gal. 6:9). For that is the time God has chosen for it; and be sure his choice, as the choice of infinite wisdom, is the best; and therefore faith sets to wait it (Isa. 28:16), 'He that believeth shall not make haste'.

Much of the beauty of any thing depends on the timing of it, and he has fixed that in all that he does (Eccles. 3:11), 'He hath made every thing beautiful in his time'.

8. The lifting up of the humble will not fail to come in the appointed and due time (Hab. 2:3). Time makes no halting, it is running day and night; so the due time is fast coming, and when it comes, it will bring the lifting up along with it. Let the humbling circumstances be ever so low, ever so hopeless, it is impossible but the lifting up from them must come in the due time.

A word, in the general, to the lifting up, abiding those that humble themselves. There is a two-fold lifting up.

A partial lifting up, competent to the humbled in time, during this life, 'I will extol thee, O Lord, for thou hast lifted me up, and hast not made my foes to rejoice over me' (Ps. 30:1). This is a lifting up in part, and but in part, not wholly; and such lifting up the humbled may expect, while in this world, but no more. These give a breathing to the weary, a change of burdens, but do not set them at perfect ease. So Israel, in the wilderness, in the midst of their many mourning times, had some singing ones (Exod. 15:1; Num. 21:17).

A total lifting up, competent to them at the end of time, at death (Luke 16:22), 'It came to pass, that the beggar died, and was carried, by the angels, into Abraham's bosom'. Then the Lord deals with them no more by parcels, but carries their relief to perfection (Heb. 12:22, 23). Then he takes off all their burdens, eases them of all their weights, and lays no more on for ever. He then lifts them up to a height they were never at before; no, not even at their highest. He sets them quite above all that is low, and therein fixes them, never to be brought down more. Now, there is a due time for both these.

For the partial lifting up. Every time is not fit for it; we are not always fit to receive comfort and ease, or a change of our burdens. God sees there are times wherein it is needful for his people to be 'in heaviness' (1 Pet. 1:6) to have their 'hearts brought down with grief' (Ps. 107:12). But then there is a time really appointed for it in the divine wisdom, when he will think it as needful to comfort them, as before to bring down, 'So that, contrarywise, ye ought rather to forgive, and comfort him, lest perhaps such a one should be swallowed up with over much sorrow' (2 Cor. 2:7). We are, in that case, in the hand of God, as in the hand of our physician, who appoints the time the drawing plaster shall continue, and when the healing plaster shall be applied, and leaves it not to the patient.

For the total lifting up. When we are sore oppressed with our burdens, we are ready to think, Oh! To be away, and set beyond them all, 'As a servant earnestly desireth the shadow, and as an hireling looketh for the reward of his work; so am I made to possess months of vanity, and wearisome nights are appointed to me' (Job 7:2, 3). But it may be fitter, for all that, that we stay awhile, and struggle with our burdens, 'Nevertheless, to abide in the flesh is more needful for you. And having this confidence, I know that I shall abide and continue with you all, for your furtherance and joy of faith' (Phil. 1:24, 25). A few days might have taken Israel out of Egypt into Canaan; but they would have been too soon there, if they had made all that speed; so they chose to spend forty years in the wilderness, till their due time of entering Canaan should come. And be sure the saints entering heaven will be convinced, that the time of it is best chosen, and there will be a beauty in that it was no sooner. And thus a lifting up is secured for the humble.

6

God Uplifts His People in Affliction

If one should assure you, when reduced to poverty, that the time would certainly come yet, that you should be rich; when sore sick, that you should not die of that disease, but certainly recover; that would help you to bear your poverty and sickness the better, and you would comfort yourselves with that prospect. However, one may continue poor, and never be rich, may be sick, and die of his disease; but whoever humble themselves under their humbling circumstances, we can assure them from the Lord's word they shall certainly, without all peradventure, be lifted up out of, and relieved from, their humbling circumstances: they shall certainly see the day of their ease and relief, when they shall remember their burdens as waters that fail. And you may be assured thereof, from the following considerations.

1. The nature of God, duly considered, ensures it, 'The Lord is merciful and gracious, slow to anger, and plenteous in mercy. He will not always chide; neither will he keep his anger forever' (Ps. 103:8, 9). The humbled soul, looking to God in Christ, may see three things, in his nature jointly securing it.

Infinite power, that can do all things. No circumstances are so low, but he can raise them; so entangling and perplexing, but he can unravel them; so hopeless, but he can remedy them, 'Is any thing too hard for the Lord?' (Gen. 18:14). Be our case what it will, it is never past reaching Him to help it. But then, it is the most proper season for him to take it in hand, when all others have given it over, 'For the Lord shall judge his people, and repent himself for his servants; when he seeth that their power is gone, and there is none shut up, or left' (Deut. 32:36).

2. Infinite goodness inclining to help. He is good and gracious in his nature (Exod. 34:6, 7). And therefore his power is a spring of comfort to them (Rom. 14:4). Men may be willing that are not able, or able that are not willing; but infinite goodness, joining infinite power in God, may ascertain the humbled of a lifting up in due time. That is a word of inconceivable sweetness, 'And we have known and believed the love that God hath unto us. God is love; and he that dwelleth in love, dwelleth in God, and God in him' (1 John 4:16). He has the bowels of a father towards the humble, 'Like as a father pitieth his children, so the Lord pitieth them that fear him' (Ps. 103:13). Yea, bowels of mercy more tender than a mother to her sucking child (Isa. 49:15). Wherefore, howbeit his wisdom may see it necessary to put them in humbling circumstances, and keep them there for a time, it is not possible he can leave them therein altogether.

Infinite wisdom, that does nothing in vain, and therefore will not needlessly keep one in humbling circumstances, 'But though he cause grief, yet will he have compassion according to the multitude of his mercies; for he doth not afflict willingly, nor grieve the children of men'

132

(Lam. 3:32, 33). God sends afflictions for humbling, as the end and design to be brought about by them; when what is obtained, and there is no more use for them that way, we may assure ourselves they will be taken off.

The Providence of God, viewed in its stated methods of procedure with its objects, ensures it. Turn your eyes which way you will on the divine Providence, you may conclude thence, that in due time the humble will be lifted up.

Observe the Providence of God, in the revolutions of the whole course of nature, day succeeding to the longest night, a summer to the winter, a waxing to a waning of the moon, a flowing to an ebbing of the sea, etc. Let not the Lord's humbled ones be idle spectators of these things: they are for our learning, 'Thus saith the Lord, which gives the sun for a light by day, and the ordinances of the moon, and of the stars for a light by night, which divideth the sea, when the waves thereof roar; the Lord of hosts is his name. If those ordinances depart from before me, saith the Lord, then the seed of Israel also shall cease from being a nation before me for ever' (Jer. 31:35-37). Will the Lord's hand keep such a steady course in the earth, sea, and visible heavens, as to bring a lifting up in them after a casting down, and only forget his humbled ones? No, by no means.

Observe the Providence of God, in the dispensations thereof, about the man Christ, the most noble and august object thereof, more valuable than a thousand worlds (Col. 2:9). Did not Providence keep this course with him, first humbling him, then exalting him, and lifting him up? First bringing him to the dust of death, in a course of sufferings thirty-three years, then exalting him to the Father's right hand in an eternity of glory? 'Who for the joy that was set before him, endured the cross, despising the shame, and is now set down at the right hand of the throne of God' (Heb. 12:2). 'And being found in fashion as a man, he humbled himself, and became obedient unto death, even the death of the cross, wherefore God also hath highly exalted him' (Phil. 2:8, 9). The exaltation could not fail to follow his humiliation, 'Ought not Christ to have suffered these things, and to enter into his glory?' (Luke 24:26). And he saw and believed it would follow, as the springing of the seed does the sowing it (John 12:24). There is a near concern the humbled in humbling circumstances have herein.

This is the pattern Providence copies after in its conduct towards you. The Father was so well pleased with this method, in the case of his own Son, that it was determined to be followed, and just copied over again in the case of all the heirs of glory (Rom. 8:29), 'For whom he did foreknow, he also did predestinate to be conformed to the image of his Son, that he "might be the first born among many brethren"'. And who would not be pleased to walk through the darkest valley treading his steps?

This is a sure pledge of your lifting up. Christ, in his state of humiliation, was considered as a public person and representative, and so is he in his exaltation. So Christ's exaltation ensures your exaltation out of your humbling circumstances, 'Thy dead men shall live, together with my dead body shall they arise; awake and sing, ye that dwell in the dust' (Isa. 26:19). 'Come and let us return unto the Lord: for he hath torn, and he will heal us, he hath smitten, and he will bind us up. After two days he will revive us: in the third day, he will raise us up, and we shall live in his sight' (Hosea 6:1, 2). 'And hath raised us up together, and made us sit together in heavenly places in Christ Jesus' (Eph. 2:6). Yea, he is gone into the state of glory for us as our forerunner. 'Whither the forerunner is for us entered, even Jesus, made an high priest for ever' (Heb. 6:20).

His humiliation was the price of your exaltation, and his exaltation a testimony of the acceptance of its payment to the full. There are no humbling circumstances ye are in, but ye would have perished in them, had not he purchased your lifting up out of them by his own humiliation (Isa. 26:19). Now his humbling grace in you is an evidence of the acceptance of his humiliation for your lifting up.

Observe the Providence of God towards the church in all ages. This has been the course the Lord has kept with her (Ps. 129:1-4). Abel was slain by wicked Cain, to the great grief of Adam and Eve, and the rest of their pious children; but then there was another seed raised up in Abel's room (Gen. 4:25). Noah and his sons were buried alive in the ark for more than a year: but then they were brought out into a New World and blessed. Abraham for many years went childless; but at length Isaac was born. Israel was long in miserable bondage in Egypt; but at length seated in the Promised Land, etc. We must be content to go by the footsteps of the flock; and if in humiliation, we shall surely follow them in exaltation too.

Observe the Providence of God in the dispensations of his grace towards his children. The general rule is, 'For God resisteth the proud, and gives grace to the humble' (1 Pet. 5:5). How are they brought into a state of grace? Is it not by a sound work of humiliation going before? (Luke 6:48). And ordinarily the greater the measure of grace designed for any, the deeper is their humiliation before, as in Paul's case. If they are to be recovered out of a backsliding case, the same method is followed so that the deepest humiliation ordinarily makes way for the greatest comfort, and the darkest hour goes before the rising of the Sun of righteousness upon them (Isa. 66:5-13).

Observe the Providence of God at length throwing down wicked men, however long they stand and prosper, 'I have seen the wicked in great power, and spreading himself like a green bay tree; yet he passed away, and lo he was not; yea, I sought him but he could not be found' (Ps. 37:35, 36). They are long green before the sun, but at length they are suddenly smitten with an east wind, and wither away; their lamp goes out with a stench, and they are put out in obscure darkness. Now, it is inconsistent with the benignity of the divine nature, to forget the humble to raise them, while he minds the proud to abase them.

The word of God puts it beyond all peradventure, which, from the beginning to the end, is the humbled saint's security for a lifting up, 'Remember the word unto thy servant, upon which thou hast caused me to hope. This is my comfort in my affliction; for thy word hath quickened me' (Ps. 119:49, 50). His word is the great letter of his name, which he will certainly cause to shine, 'For thou hast magnified thy word above all thy name' (Ps. 138:2); and in all generations hast been safely relied on (Ps. 12:6). Consider:

1. The doctrines of the word, which teach faith and hope for the time, and the happy issue which the exercise of these graces will have. The whole current of scripture, to those in humbling circumstances, is, 'not to cast away their confidence, but to hope to the end'; and that for this good reason, that 'it shall not be in vain'. See Psalm 27:14, 'Wait on the Lord; be of good courage, and he shall strengthen thine heart; wait, I say, on the Lord'. And compare Romans 9:33, Isaiah 49:23, 'For they shall not be ashamed that wait for me'.

2. The promises of the word, whereby heaven is expressly engaged for a lifting up to those that humble themselves in humbling circumstances, 'Humble yourselves in the sight of the Lord, and he shall lift you up' (James 4:10). 'And he that humbleth himself shall be exalted' (Matt. 23:12). It may take a time to prepare them for lifting up, but that being done, it is secured, 'Lord, thou hast heard the desire of the humble; thou wilt prepare their heart; thou wilt cause thine ear to hear' (Ps. 10:17). They have his word for deliverance (Ps. 50:15). And though they may seem to be forgotten, they shall not be always so; the time of their deliverance will come. 'For the needy shall not always be forgotten: the expectation of the poor shall not perish forever (Ps. 9:18). 'He will regard the prayer of the destitute, and not despise their prayer' (Ps. 102:17).

3. The examples of the word sufficiently confirming the truth of the doctrines and promises, 'For whatsoever things were written aforetime, were written for our learning; that we through patience and comfort of the scriptures might have hope' (Rom. 15:4). In the doctrines and promises the lifting up is proposed to our faith, to be reckoned on the credit of God's word; but, in the examples it is, in the case of others, set before our eyes to be seen. 'Behold we count them happy which endure. Ye have heard of the patience of Job, and have seen the end of the Lord; that the Lord is very pitiful, and of tender mercy' (James 5:11). There we see it in the case of Abraham, Job, David, Paul, and other saints; but above all, in the case of the man, Christ.

4. The intercession of Christ, joining the prayers and cries of his humbled people, in their humbling circumstances, ensures a lifting up for them at length. Be it so, that the proud cry not when he binds them; yet his own

humbled ones will certainly cry unto him, 'Deep calleth unto deep, at the noise of thy water spouts; all thy waves and thy billows are gone over me. Yet the Lord will command his loving-kindness in the daytime, and in the night his song shall be with me, and my prayer unto the God of my life' (Ps. 42:7, 8). And though unbelievers may soon be outwearied, and give it over altogether, surely believers will not do so; but though they may, in a fit of temptation, lay it by as hopeless, they will find themselves obliged to take it up again, 'Then I said, I will not make mention of him, nor speak any more in his name. But his word was in mine heart as a burning fire shut up in my bones and I was weary with forbearing, and I could not stay' (Jer. 20:9). They will cry, night and day, unto him (Luke 18:7), knowing no time for giving it over till they be lifted up. 'Mine eye trickleth down, and ceaseth not, and behold from heaven' (Lam. 3:49, 50). Now, Christ's intercession being joined with these cries, there cannot fail to be a lifting up.

Christ's intercession is certainly joined with the cries and prayers of the humbled in their humbling circumstances, 'And another angel came and stood at the altar, having a golden censer: and there was given unto him much incense, that he should offer it with the prayers of all saints upon the golden altar which was before the throne' (Rev. 8:3). They are by the Spirit helped to groan for relief (Rom. 8:26) and the prayers and groans, which are through the Spirit, are certainly to be made effectual by the intercession of the Son (James 5:16). And ye may know they are by the Spirit, if so be ye are helped to continue praying, hoping for your suit at last on the ground of God's word of promise; for nature's praying is a pool that will dry up in a long drought. The Spirit of prayer is the lasting spring

(John 4:14; Ps. 138:3), 'In the day when I cried, thou answeredst me; and strengthenedst me with strength in my soul'. Truly there is an intercession in heaven, on account of the humbling circumstances of the humble ones. 'Then the angel of the Lord answered and said, "O Lord of hosts, how long wilt thou not have mercy on Jerusalem, and on the cities of Judah, against which thou hast had indignation these threescore and ten years?"' (Zech. 1:12). How then can they miss of a lifting up in due time?

Christ is in deep earnest in his intercession for his people in their humbling circumstances. Some will speak a good word in favour of the helpless, that will be little concerned whether they speed or not. But our Intercessor is in earnest on behalf of his humbled ones: for he is touched with sympathy in their case, 'In all their affliction he was afflicted' (Isa. 63:9). A most tender sympathy, 'For he that toucheth you, toucheth the apple of his eye' (Zech. 2:8). He has their case upon his heart, where he is in the holy place in the highest heavens (Exod. 28:29), and he keeps an exact account of the time of their humbling circumstances, be it as long as it will (Zech. 1:12). Moreover, it is his own business; the lifting up which they are to have is a thing that is secured to him in the promises made to him on the account of his blood shed for them (Ps. 139:33-36). So not only are they looking on earth, but the man Christ is in heaven looking for the accomplishment of these promises, 'But this man, after he had offered one sacrifice for sins, for ever sat down on the right hand of God; from henceforth expecting till his enemies be made his footstool' (Heb. 10:12, 13). How is it possible, then, that he should be balked? Moreover, these humbling circumstances are his own sufferings still, though not in his person, yet in his members, 'Who now rejoice in my sufferings for you, and fill up that which is behind of the afflictions of Christ in my flesh, for his body's sake, which is the church' (Col. 1:24). Wherefore there is all ground to conclude he is in deep earnest. Again:

His intercession is always effectual, 'And I know that thou hearest me always' (John 11:42). It cannot miss to be so, because he is the Father's well-beloved Son; his intercession has a plea of justice for the ground of it, 'We have an advocate with the Father, Jesus Christ the righteous' (1 John 2:1). Moreover, he has all power in heaven and earth lodged in him (Matt. 28:18). And, finally, he and his Father are one, and there will be one. So, both Christ and his Father do will the lifting up of the humble ones, but yet only in the due time.

I now proceed to a more particular view of the point. And we will consider the lifting up as brought about in time, which is the partial lifting up.

This lifting up does not take place in every case of a child of God. One may be humbled in humbling circumstances, from which he is not to get a lifting up in time. We would not from the promise presently conclude, that we being humbled under our humbling circumstances, shall certainly be taken out of them, and freed from them ere we get to the end of our journey. For it is certain, there are some, such as our imperfections, and sinfulness, and mortality, we can by no means be rid of while in this world. And there are particular humbling circumstances the Lord may bring about one, and keep about him, till he goes down to the grave, while, in the mean time, he may lift up another from the same. Heman was pressed down all along from his youth (Ps. 88:15), others all their lifetime (Heb. 2:15).

Objection: 'If that be the case, what comes of the promise of lifting up? Where is the lifting up, if one may go to the grave under the weight?'

Answer: Were there no life after this, there would be ground for that objection; but since there is another life, there is none in it at all. In the other life the promise will be accomplished to the humbled, as it was (Luke 16:22). Consider that the great term for accomplishing the promises, is the other life, not this. 'These all died in the faith, not having received the promises, but having seen them afar off, and were persuaded of them, and embraced them' (Heb. 11:13). And that whatever accomplishment of the promise is here, it is not of the nature of a stock, but of a sample or a pledge.

Question: 'But then, may we not give over praying for the lifting up, in that case?'

Answer: We do not know when that is our case; for a case may be past all hope in our eyes, and the eyes of others, in which God designs a lifting up in time, as in Job's, 'What is my strength that I should hope; and what is mine end that I should prolong my life?' (6:11). But, be it as it will, we should never give over praying for the lifting up, since it will certainly come to all that pray in faith for it; if not here, yet hereafter. The promise is sure, and that is the commandment; so such praying cannot miss of a happy issue at length, 'Call upon me in the day of trouble; I will deliver thee, and thou shalt glorify me' (Ps. 50:15). The whole life of a Christian is a praying, waiting life, to encourage whereunto all temporal deliverances are given as pledges, 'And not only they, but ourselves also, which have the first fruits of the Spirit; even we ourselves groan within ourselves, waiting for the adoption, to wit, the redemption

141

of our body' (Rom. 8:23). And whoso observes that full lifting up at death to be at hand, must certainly rise, if he has given over his case as hopeless.

However, there are some cases wherein this lifting up does take place. God gives his people some notable liftings up, even in time raising them out of remarkably humbling circumstances. The storm is changed into a calm, and they remember it as waters that fail (Ps. 40:1-4).

Some may be in humbling circumstances very long, and sore and hopeless, and yet a lifting up may be abiding them, of a much longer continuance. This is sometimes the case with the children of God, who are set to bear the yoke in their youth, as it was with Joseph and David; and of them that get it laid on them in their middle age, as it was with Job, who could not be less than forty years old at his trouble's coming, but after it, lived one hundred and forty (Job 42:16). God by such methods prepares man for peculiar usefulness.

Others may be in humbling circumstances long and sore, and quite hopeless in the ordinary course of Providence, yet they may get a lifting up, ere they come to their journey's end. The life of some of God's children is like a cloudy and rainy day, wherein, in the evening, the sun breaks out from under the clouds, shines fair and clear a little, and then sets. 'And it shall come to pass in that day, that the light shall not be clear, nor dark. But it shall come to pass, that at evening time it shall be light' (Zech. 14:6, 7). Such was the case of Jacob in his old age, brought in honour and comfort into Egypt unto his son, and then died.

Yet, whatever lifting up they get in this life, they will never want some weights hanging about them for their humbling. They may have their singing times, but their songs while in this world, will be mixed with groanings,

'For we that are in this tabernacle do groan, being burdened' (2 Cor. 5:4). The unmixed dispensation is reserved for the other world; but this will be a wilderness unto the end, where there will be howling, with the most joyful notes.

All the lifting up which the humbled meet with now are pledges, and but pledges and samples of the great lifting up, abiding [with] them on the other side. And they should look on them so, 'And I will give her her vineyards from thence, and the valley of Achor for a door of hope; and she shall sing there as in the days of her youth, and as in the day when she came up out of the land of Egypt.' (Hosea 2:15). Our Lord is now leading his people through the wilderness, and the manna and the water of the rock are earnests of the milk and honey flowing in the promised land. They are not yet come home to their Father's house, but they are travelling on the road, and Christ their elder brother with them, who bears their expenses, takes them into inns by the way, as it were, and refreshes them with partial liftings up; after which, they must get to the road again. But that entertainment by the way is a pledge of the full entertainment he will afford them when they come home.

Objection: 'But people may get a lifting up in time that yet is no pledge of a lifting up on the other side: How shall I know it then to be a pledge?'

Answer: That lifting up which comes by the promises, is certainly a pledge of the full lifting up in the other world; for, as the other life is the proper time of the accomplishing of the promises, so we may be sure, that when God once begins to clear his bond, he will certainly hold on till it is fully cleared. 'The Lord will perfect that which concerneth me' (Ps. 138:8). So we may say, as Naomi to Ruth, upon her receiving the six measures of barley from Boaz (Ruth 3:18), 'He will not be in rest until he have finished the thing this day'. There are liftings up that come by common providence, and these indeed are single, and not pledges of more; but the promise chains mercies together, so that one got is a pledge of another to come, yea, of the whole chain to the end (2 Sam. 5:12).

Question: 'But how shall I know the lifting up to come by the way of the promise?'

Answer: That which comes by the way of the promise, comes in the low way of humiliation, the high way of faith, or believing the promise, and the long way of waiting hope and patient continuance, 'Be patient therefore, brethren, unto the coming of the Lord. Behold the husbandman waiteth for the precious fruit of the earth, and hath long patience for it until he receive the early and latter rain' (James 5:7). Humility prepares for the accomplishment of the promise, faith sucks the breast of it, and patient waiting hangs by the breast till the milk come abundantly.

But no lifting up of God's children here are any more than pledges of lifting up. God gives worldly men their stock here, but his children get nothing but a sample of theirs here (Ps. 17:14). Even as the servant at the term gets his fee in a round sum, while the young heir gets nothing but a few pence for spending money. The truth is, this same spending money is more valuable than the world's stock, 'Thou hast put gladness in my heart, more than in the time that their corn and their wine increased' (Ps. 4:7). But though it is better than that, and their services too, and more worth than all their waiting, yet it is below the honour of their God to put them off with it, 'But now they desire a better country, that is, an heavenly; wherefore God is not ashamed to be called their God; for he hath prepared for them a city' (Heb. 11:16).

We shall now consider what they will get by this lifting up promised to the humbled:

1. They will get a removal of their humbling circumstances. God having tried them awhile, and humbled them, and brought down their hearts, will, at length, take off their burden, remove the weight so long hung on them, and so take them off that part of their trial joyfully, and let them get up their back long bowed down; and this one of two ways.

Either in kind, by a total removal of the burden. Such a lifting Job got, when the Lord turned back his captivity, increased again his family and substance, which had both been desolated. David, when Saul his persecutor fell in battle, and he was brought to the kingdom after many a weary day, expecting one day to fall by his hand. It is easy with our God to make such turns in the most humbling circumstances.

Or in equivalent, or as good, removing the weight of the burden, that though it remains, it presses them no more, 'And he said unto me, "My grace is sufficient for thee, for my strength is made perfect in weakness." Most gladly, therefore, will I rather glory in my infirmities, that the power of Christ may rest upon me. Therefore, I take pleasure in infirmities' (2 Cor. 12:9, 10). Though they are not got to the shore, yet their head is no more under the water, but lifted up. David speaks feelingly of such a lifting up, 'For in the time of trouble he shall hide me in his pavilion; in the secret of his tabernacle shall he hide me; he shall set me upon a rock. And now shall mine head be lifted up above mine enemies round about me; therefore will I offer in his tabernacle sacrifices of joy; I will sing, yea, I will sing praises unto the Lord' (Ps. 27:5, 6). Such had the three Hebrews in the fiery furnace, the fire burnt, but it could burn nothing of them but their bonds; they had the warmth and light of it, but nothing of the scorching heat.

2. A comfortable sight of the acceptance of their prayers, put up in their humbling circumstances. While prayers are not answered, but trouble continued, they are apt to think they are not accepted or regarded in heaven, because there is no alteration in their case, 'If I had called, and he had answered me, yet would I not believe that he had hearkened unto my voice, for he breaketh me with a tempest' (Job 9:16, 17). But that is a mistake; they are accepted immediately, though not answered, 'And this is the confidence we have in him, that if we ask anything according to his will, he heareth us' (1 John 5:14). The Lord does with them as a father, with the letters coming thick from his son abroad, reads them one by one with pleasure, and carefully lays them up to be answered at his convenience. And when the answer comes, the son will know how acceptable they were to his father (Matt. 15:28).

3. A heart-satisfying answer of their prayers, so that they shall not only get the thing, but see they have it as an answer of prayer; and they will put a double value on the mercy (1 Sam. 2:1). Accepted prayers may be very long of answering, many years, as in Abraham and David's case, but they cannot miscarry of an answer at length (Ps. 9:18). The time will come when God will tell out to them, according to the promise, that they shall change their note, and say, 'I love the Lord, because he hath heard my voice, and my supplication' (Ps. 116:1): looking on their lifting up as bearing the signature of the hand of a prayer-hearing God.

4. Full satisfaction, as to the conduct of Providence, in all the steps of the humbling circumstances, and the delay of the lifting up, however perplexing these were before (Rev. 15:3). Standing on the shore, and looking back to what they have passed through, they will be made to say,

'He hath done all things well'. Those things that are bitter to Christians in passing through, are very sweet in the reflection on them; so is Samson's riddle verified in their experience.

5. They get the lifting up, together with the interest for the time they lay out of it. When God pays his bonds of promises, he pays both principal and interest together; the mercy is increased according to the time they waited, and the expenses and hardships sustained, during the dependence of the process. The fruits of common providence are soon ripe, soon rotten; but the fruit of the promise is often long a ripening, but then it is durable: and the longer it is a ripening, it is the more valuable when it comes. Abraham and Sarah waited for the promise about ten years, at length they thought on a way to hasten it (Gen. 16). That soon took, in the birth of Ishmael, but he was not the promised son. They were coming into extreme old age ere the promise brought forth (Gen. 18:11). But when it came, they got it with an addition of the renewing of their ages (Gen. 21:7 and 25:1). The most valuable of all the promises was the longest in fulfilling, namely, the promise of Christ that was [for] four thousand years.

6. The spiritual enemies, that flew thick about them in the time of the darkness of the humbling circumstances, will be scattered at this lifting up in the promise, 'And Hannah prayed and said, "My heart rejoiceth in the Lord, my mouth is enlarged over mine enemies. They that were full have hired out themselves for bread, and they that were hungry ceased"' (1 Sam. 2:1, 5). Formidable was Pharaoh's host behind the Israelites, while they had the Red Sea before them; but when they were through the sea, they saw the Egyptians dead on the shore (Exod. 14:30). Such

a sight will they that humble themselves under humbling circumstances get of their spiritual enemies, when the time comes for their lifting up.

We come now to the due time of this lifting up. That is a natural question of those who are in humbling circumstances, 'Watchman, what of the night?' (Isa. 21:11, 12). And we cannot answer it to the humbled soul, but in the general.

The lifting up of the humbled will not be long [delayed], considering the weight of the matter; that is to say, considering the worth and value of the lifting up of the humble; when it comes it can by no means be reckoned long to the time of it. When you sow your corn in the fields, though it does not ripen so soon as some garden-seeds, but you wait three months or so, you do not think the harvest long a coming, considering the value of the crop. This view the apostle takes of the lifting up in humbling circumstances, 'For our light affliction, which is but for a moment, worketh for us a far more exceeding and eternal weight of glory' (2 Cor. 4:17). So that a believer, looking on the promise with an eye of faith, and perceiving its accomplishment, and the worth of it when accomplished, may wonder it is come so shortly. Therefore, it is determined to be a time that comes soon (Luke 18:7, 8), soon in respect of its weight and worth.

When the time comes, it and only it will appear the due time. To every thing there is a season, and a great part of wisdom lies in discerning it, and doing things in this season thereof. And we may be sure infinite Wisdom cannot miss the season, by mistaking it, 'He is a rock, his work is perfect; for all his ways are judgment' (Deut. 32:4). But whatever God doth, will abide the strictest examination, in that, as all other points, 'I know that whatsoever God doth, it shall be for ever; nothing can be put to it, nor any thing taken from it: and God doth it that men may fear before him' (Eccles. 3:14). It is true, many times appear to us as the due time for lifting up, which yet really is not so, because there are some circumstances hid from us, which render that season unfit for the thing. Hence, 'My time is not yet come, but your time is always ready' (John 7:6). But when all the circumstances, always foreknown of God, shall come to be opened out, and laid together before us, we shall then see the lifting up is come in the time most for the honour of God and our good, and that it would not have done so well sooner.

When the time comes that is really the due time, the proper time for the lifting up a child of God from his humbling circumstances, it will not be put off one moment longer, 'At the end it shall speak, it will surely come, it will not tarry' (Hab. 2:3). Though it tarry, it will not linger, nor be put off to another time. O what rest of heart would the firm faith of this afford us! There is not a child of God but would, with the utmost earnestness, protest against a lifting up before the due time, as against an unripe fruit cast to him by an angry father which would set his teeth on edge. Since it is so then, could we firmly believe this point, that it will undoubtedly come in the due time, without losing of a minute, it would afford a sound rest. It must be so, because God has said it; were the case ever so hopeless, were mountains of difficulties lying in the way of it, at the appointed time it will blow (Hebrew), (Hab. 2:3). A metaphor from the wind, rising in a moment after a dead calm.

The humbling circumstances are ordinarily carried to the utmost point of hopelessness before the lifting up. The knife was at Isaac's throat before the voice was heard, 'For we would not, brethren, have you ignorant of our trouble which came to us in Asia, that we were pressed out of measure, above strength, insomuch that we despaired even of life; but we had the sentence of death in ourselves, that we should not trust in ourselves, but in God, which raiseth the dead' (2 Cor. 1:8, 9). Things soon seem to us arrived at that point; such is the hastiness of our spirits. But things may have far to go down after we think they are at the foot of the hill. And we are almost as little competent judges of the point of hopelessness, as of the due time of lifting up. But generally God carries his people's humbling circumstances downward, still downward, till they come to that point.

Herein God is holding the same course which he held in the case of the man Christ, the beloved pattern copied after, in all the dispensations of Providence towards the church, and every particular believer (Rom. 8:29). He was all along a man of sorrows; as his time went on, the waters swelled more, till he was brought to the dust of death; then he was buried, and the grave-stone sealed; which done, the world thought they were quit of him, and he would trouble them no more. But they quite mistook it; then, and not till then, was the due time for lifting him up. And the most remarkable lifting up that his people get, are fashioned after this grand pattern.

Another end which Providence aims at, is to carry the believer clean off his own, and all created foundations, to fix his trust and hope in the Lord alone, 'That we should not trust in ourselves, but in God which raiseth the dead' (2 Cor. 1:9). The life of a Christian here is designed to be a life of faith; and though faith may act more easily when it has some help from sense, yet it certainly acts most nobly when it acts in opposition to sense. Then is it pure faith, when it stands only on its own native legs, the power and word of God (Rom. 4:19, 20), 'And being not weak in faith, he considered not his own body now dead - neither yet the deadness of Sarah's womb. He staggered not at the promise of God through unbelief; but was strong in faith, giving glory to God.' And thus it must do, when matters are carried to the utmost point of hopelessness.

Again, due preparation of the heart, for the lifting up out of the humbling circumstances, goes before the due time of that lifting up, according to the promise. It is not so in every lifting up; the liftings up of common providences are not so critically managed; men will have them, will wait for them no longer, and God flings them in anger, ere they are prepared for them, 'I gave thee a king in mine anger' (Hosea 13:11). They can by no means abide the trial, and God takes them off as reprobate silver that is not able to abide it (Jer. 6:29, 30).

This due preparation consists in a due humiliation (Ps. 10:17). And it often takes much work to bring about this, which is another point that we are very incompetent judges of. We should have thought Job was brought very low in his spirit, by the providence of God bruising him on the one hand, and his friends on the other, for a long time: yet, after all that he had endured both ways, God saw it necessary to speak to him himself, for his humiliation (ch. 38:1). By that speech of God himself, he was brought to his knees (ch. 40:4, 5). And we should have thought he was then sufficiently humbled, and perhaps he thought so too. But God saw a further degree of humiliation necessary, and therefore begins again to speak for his humiliation, which at length laid him in the dust (ch. 42:5, 6). And when he was thus prepared for lifting up, he got it.

There are six things, I conceive, belong to this humiliation, preparatory to lifting up.

1. A deep sense of sinfulness and unworthiness of being lifted up at all, 'Behold I am vile, what shall I answer thee? I will lay mine hand upon my mouth' (Job 40:4). People may be long in humbling circumstances, ere they be brought this length; even good men are much prejudiced in their own behalf, and may so far forget themselves as to think God deals his favours unequally, and is mighty severe on them more than others. Elihu marks this fault in Job, under his humbling circumstances (Job 33:8-12). And I believe it will be found, there is readily a greater keenness to vindicate our own honour from the imputation the humbling circumstances seem to lay upon it, than to vindicate the honour of God in the justice and equity of the dispensation. The blindness of an ill-natured world, still ready to suspect the worst causes for humbling circumstances, as if the greatest sufferers were surely the greatest sinners (Luke 13:4), gives a handle for this bias of the corrupt nature. But God is a jealous God, and when he appears sufficiently to humble, he will cause the matter of our honour to give way to the vindication of his.

2. A resignation to the divine pleasure as to the time of lifting up. God gives the promise, leaving the time blank as to us. Our time is always ready, and we rashly fill it up at our own hand. God does not keep our time, because it is not the due time. Hence we are ready to think his word fails; whereas it is but our own rash conclusion from it that fails, 'I said in my haste, All men are liars' (Ps. 116:11). Several of the saints have suffered much by this means, and thereby learned to let alone filling up that blank. The

first promise was thus used by believing Eve (Gen. 4:1). Another promise was so by believing Abraham, after about ten years' waiting (Gen. 16).

If this be the case of any child of God, let them not be discouraged upon it, thinking they were overly rash in applying the promise to themselves; they were only so in applying the time to the promise, a mistake that saints in all ages have made, which they repented, and saw the folly of, and let alone that point for the time to come; and then the promise was fulfilled in its own due time. Let them in such circumstances go and do likewise, leaving the time entirely to the Lord.

3. An entire resignation as to the way and manner of bringing it about. We are ready to do, as to the way of accomplishing the promise, just as with the time of it, to set a particular way for the Lord's working of it; and if that be not kept, the proud heart is stumbled, 'But Naaman was wroth, and he went away, and said, "Behold, I thought he will surely come out to me, and stand and call on the name of the Lord his God, and strike his hand over the place"' (2 Kings 5:11). But the Lord will have his people broken off from that too, that they shall prescribe no way to him, but leave it to him entirely, as in that case (v. 14), 'He went down and dipped himself seven times in Jordan, according to the saying of the man of God, and he was clean'. The compass of our knowledge of ways and means is very narrow, as, if one is blocked up, ofttimes we cannot see another; but our God knows many ways of relief, where we know but one or none at all; and it is very usual for the Lord to bring the lifting up of his people in a way they had no view to, after repeated disappointments from those quarters whence they had great expectation.

4. Resignation as to the degree of the lifting up, yea, and as to the very being of it in time. The Lord will have his people weaned so, that however hasty they have sometimes been, that they behoved to be so soon lifted up, and could no longer bear, they shall be brought at length to set no time at all, but submit to go to the grave under their weight, if it seem good in the Lord's eyes; and in that case they will be brought to be content with any measure of it in time, without prescribing how much, 'If I shall find favour in the eyes of the Lord, he will bring me again - But if he thus say, "I have no delight in thee"; behold, here am I, let him do as seemeth good unto him' (2 Sam. 15:25, 26).

5. The continuing of praying and waiting on the Lord in the case, 'Praying always with all prayer and supplication in the Spirit, and watching thereunto with all perseverance' (Eph. 6:18). It is pride of heart, and an unsubdued spirit, that makes people give over praying and waiting, because their humbling circumstances are lengthened out time after time (2 Kings 6:33). But due humility, going before the lifting up, brings men into that temper, to pray, wait, and hang on resolutely, setting no time for the giving it over till the lifting up come, whether in time or eternity (Lam. 3:49, 50).

6. Mourning under mismanagement of the trial, 'Therefore have I uttered that I understood not, things too wonderful for me, which I knew not' (Job 42:3). The proud heart dwells and expatiates on the man's sufferings in the trial, and casts out all the folds of the trial, on that side, and views them again and again. But when the Spirit of God comes duly to humble, in order to lift up, he will cause the man to pass, in a sort, the suffering side of the trial, and turn his eyes on his own conduct in it, ransack it, judge himself impartially, and condemn himself, so that his

154

mouth will be stopt. This is that humility that goes before the lifting up in time, in the way of the promise.

We proceed to consider the lifting up as brought about at the end of time, in the other world. And a word as to the nature of this lifting up: concerning this we shall say these five things:

There is a certainty of this lifting up, in all cases of the humbled under humbling circumstances. Though one cannot, in every case, make them sure of a lifting up in time, yet they may be assured, be the case what it may, they will, without all peradventure, get a lifting up on the other side, 'For we know, that if our earthly house of this tabernacle were dissolved, we have a building of God, an house not made with hands, eternal in the heavens' (2 Cor. 5:1). Though God's humble children may both breakfast and dine on bread of adversity, and water of affliction, they will be sure to sup sweetly and plentifully. And the believing expectation of the latter might serve to qualify the former, and make them easy under it.

It will be a perfect lifting up (Heb. 12:23). They will be perfectly delivered out of their particular trials, and special furnace, be what it will, that made them weary many a day. Lazarus was then delivered from his poverty and sores, and lying at the rich man's gate (Luke 16:22), and fully delivered. Yea, they will get a lifting up from all their humbling circumstances together. All imperfections will then be at an end, inferiority in relations, contradictions, afflictions, uncertainty, and sin. If it was long in coming, there will be a blessed moment when they shall get altogether.

They will not only be raised out of their low condition, but they will be set up on high, as Joseph; not only brought out of prison, but made ruler over the land of Egypt. And they will be lifted up into a high place, 'The beggar died, and was carried by the angels into Abraham's bosom' (Luke 16:22). Now they are at best but in a low place, upon this earth; there they will be seated in the highest heavens (Phil. 1:23 with Eph. 4:10). Often, in their humbling circumstances, they are obliged now to embrace dunghills; then they will be set with Christ on his throne, 'To him that overcometh will I grant to sit with me on my throne' (Rev. 3:21). Though they now cleave to the earth, and men say, 'Bow down, that we may pass over you', they will then be settled in the heavenly mansions, above the sun, moon, and stars. They will also be lifted up into a high state and condition, a state of perfection. Out of all their troubles and uneasiness, they will be set in a state of rest; from their mean and inglorious condition, they will be advanced into a state of glory; their burdened and sorrowful life will be succeeded with a fullness of joy; and, for their humbling circumstances, they will be clothed with eternal glory and honour.

It will be a final lifting up, after which there will be no more casting down for ever (Rev. 7:16). When we get a lifting up in time, we are apt to imagine fondly we are at the end of our trials; but we soon find we are too hasty in our conclusions, and the cloud returns, 'In my prosperity I said, I shall never be moved. Thou didst hide thy face, and I was troubled' (Ps. 30: 6, 7). But then indeed the trial is quite over, the fight is at an end, and then is the time of the retribution and triumph.

There will not be the least uneasiness remaining from the humbling circumstances, but, on the contrary, they will have a glorious and desirable effect. I make no question but the saints will have the remembrance of the humbling circumstances they were under there below. Did the rich man in hell remember his having five brethren on the earth, how sumptuously he fared, how Lazarus sat at his gate; and can we doubt but the saints will remember perfectly their heavy trials? (Rev. 6:10.) But then they will remember them as waters that fail; as the man recovered to health remembers his tossing on the sick bed; and that is a way of remembering that sweetens the present state of health beyond what otherwise it would be. Certainly the shore of the Red Sea was the place that, of all places, was the fittest to help the Israelites to sing in the highest key. And the humbling circumstances of saints on the earth will be of the same use to them in heaven (Rev. 15:3).

God's Appointed Time for our Lifting Up.
A word to the due time of this lifting up. There is a particular, definite time for it in every saint's case, which is the due time, but it is hid from us. We can only say in general:

1. Then is the due time for it, when our work we have to do in this world is over. God has appointed to every one his task, fight, trial, and work; and, till that is done, we are in a sort immortal (John 9:4 and 11:9). That work is:

Doing work: work set to us, by the great Master to be done for the honour of God, and the good of our fellow-creatures (Eccles. 9:10). We must be content to be doing on, even in our humbling circumstances, till that be done out. It is not the due time for that lifting up, till we are at the end of that work, and so have served our generation.

And it is suffering work. There is a certain portion of suffering that is allotted for the mystical body; the head has divided to the several members their proportions thereof; and it is not the due time for that lifting up, till we have exhausted the share thereof allotted to us. Paul looked on his life as a going on in that (Col. 1:24).

2. When that lifting up comes, we shall see it is come exactly in the due time; that it was well it was neither sooner or later. For though heaven is always better than earth, and that it would be better for us, absolutely speaking, to be in heaven than on earth, yet certainly there is a time wherein it is better, for the honour of God, and his service, that we be on the earth than in heaven, 'Nevertheless, to abide in the flesh is more needful for you' (Phil. 1:24). And it will be no grief of heart to them when there, that they were so long in their humbling circumstances, and were not brought sooner.

Use (application): Let not then the humble cast away their confidence, whatever their humbling circumstances be; let them assure themselves there will come a lifting up to them at length; if not here, yet to be sure hereafter. Let them keep this in their view, and comfort themselves with it, for God has said it, 'The needy shall not always be forgotten' (Ps. 9:18). If the night were ever so long, the morning will come at length.

Let patience have her perfect work. The husbandman waits for the return of his seed, the merchant for the return of his ships, the store-master for what he calls year-time, when he draws in the produce of his flocks. All these have long patience, and why should not the Christian too have patience, and patiently wait for the time appointed for his lifting up?

You have heard much of the Crook in the Lot; the excellency of humbleness of spirit in a low lot, beyond pride of spirit, though joined with a high one. You have been called to humble yourselves in your humbling circumstances, and